LESSONS IN LOVING

DEVELOPING RELATIONSHIP SKILLS

Philip St. Romain

LIGUORI
PUBLICATIONS

One Liguori Drive
Liguori, Missouri 63057-9999
(314) 464-2500

Imprimi Potest:
Stephen T. Palmer, C.SS.R.
Provincial, St. Louis Province
The Redemptorists

Imprimatur:
Monsignor Maurice F. Byrne
Vice Chancellor, Archdiocese of St. Louis

ISBN 0-89243-296-9
Library of Congress Catalog Card Number: 88-82309

TABLE OF CONTENTS

INTRODUCTION

Recently a woman came to see me about her fifteen-year-old daughter. Julie was only in the sixth grade and her mother was afraid she would quit school when she turned sixteen (which Louisiana law permits). "How will I ever convince her to stay on and get her high school diploma?" she asked in desperation.

What could I say? Even if Julie passed every grade level — which was doubtful — she would not get her diploma until she was twenty-one. There is no way she'll stay on that long, I thought. "Perhaps she will drop out, then enter adult education when she is ready," I suggested.

"Oh, I don't know," the mother persisted, clearly distraught. "I just don't want my daughter to be a failure."

"Lots of youngsters who drop out find a way to make it," I consoled. "What sorts of things can she do for a living?"

The response I got startled me. As it turned out, Julie had already organized a baby-sitting cooperative in her town. She had attended training sessions at her church and then had extended the training to several teenage girls. They already had more work than they could handle, so Julie was beginning to think of expanding her staff. She was even hoping to open a day-care center in the near future. This girl may not have been college material, but it was clear to me that she was no failure. I let her mother know this, and she began talking about Julie's future with less anxiety.

On the other hand there was Jeff, a fifteen-year-old who committed suicide on the campus of a local high school. Jeff was a bright boy; he made A's and B's on his report card. There's no doubt that he could have made it in college. But Jeff was very shy and had always struggled with friendships. When his first serious

5

girl friend told him she would like to date other boys, Jeff simply could not cope with it. At lunch on the following day, he ran up to her, pulled a pistol from his jacket, and shot himself in the head.

Similar stories about adults could be told, but these two examples from the lives of young people have been used because it is among youth that we most clearly observe some of the deepest struggles in American society. It seems that we Americans associate success during the early years with good grades, physical appearance, and later with getting ahead and staying there. As we grow older, success is associated with money, property, titles, and physical beauty. In pursuit of their goals, however, many married couples have trouble keeping their marriages together. Parent-child relationships also seem to be strained to the breaking point. Good, stable friendships also seem hard to come by.

Can anything be done to remedy this situation? Dr. Howard Gardner of Harvard University has written a book on human potential called *Frames of Mind: The Theory of Multiple Intelligences*, (Basic Books, 1983). According to Dr. Gardner, there are seven intelligences, or clusters of talents which people are capable of learning. He defines intelligence as "the ability to solve problems, or to create products, that are valued within one or more cultural settings." To Gardner's seven intelligences I have added two more, making a total of nine.

THE NINE INTELLIGENCES

1. **Linguistic:** Facility with words.

2. **Musical:** Gift of handling pitch, rhythm, and timbre.

3. **Logical-mathematical:** Ability to comprehend the cause-effect relationship between objects and concepts.

4. **Spatial:** Capability of perceiving the visual world accurately and re-creating aspects of visual experiences.

5. **Body-kinesthetic:** Facility to control bodily motions and capacity to handle objects skillfully.

6. **Intrapersonal:** Facility to discriminate among different feelings and, eventually, to label them and understand their relationship to other psychic processes.

7. **Interpersonal:** Talent for reading the intentions and desires — even when hidden — of other individuals and to act upon this knowledge.

    (The above seven scientific criteria for identifying intelligence are described more fully in Chapters One Through Four in *Frames of Mind*. I have added the following two.)

8. **Practical:** Knack of making good judgments (knowing how to handle affairs of life). This is also described by Dr. Robert Sternberg in his book, *Beyond I.Q.*, (Cambridge University Press, 1984).

9. **Mystical:** Wisdom to sense God's presence in life and a discerning awareness of how to conform one's will with the will of God.

All persons have the potential to grow in each of these nine areas, but some are more skilled in certain areas than in others. Consider Julie and Jeff, for example. Julie was obviously weak in linguistic and logical-mathematical skills, but there's no doubt she was strong in practical, intrapersonal, and interpersonal intelligence (which were apparently Jeff's weak points). Despite her difficulties in school, Julie's relationship skills will bring her a much happier life than will all Ph.D.s who fall short in these areas. In addition, I believe that a certain amount of mystical intelligence is necessary for finding peace in this world. Even gregarious and congenial souls like Julie will require a bit of mystical intelligence to help sustain their personal skills.

Gardner observes that each intelligence is most appropriately expressed and tested in its own medium. For example, music must be tested with the instrument and not with a multiple-choice test; body-kinesthetic intelligence is tested on the gym floor and not with a slide rule. Interpersonal intelligence is tested in people's friendships and families. Mystical intelligence is tested in the struggles with life's higher meaning. There are tremendous implications here for the manner in which people are screened for jobs by using various kinds of tests.

It is obvious that today's schools do not address the full range of human potential. (That they will one day do so seems to be one of Gardner's hopes.) Most schools emphasize linguistic and logical-mathematical intelligence; the remaining seven are either electives or extracurriculars. Even in private religious schools, it is debatable that mystical intelligence is being taught. The typical religion class does not foster mystical intelligence, but instead provides information about God, the Bible, and the Church — information that is largely of a linguistic and logical/conceptual nature. As for the intra- and interpersonal intelligences, the assumption seems to be that these are learned automatically through involvements in a family, classroom, or peer group. Judging by the quality of interpersonal relationships among many today, it is obvious that more needs to be done.

IMPORTANCE OF RELATIONSHIP SKILLS

Intrapersonal and interpersonal relationship skills enable us to meet our emotional and social needs (acceptance, validation, affirmation, security, and intimacy). If we do not learn to meet these needs, we will experience one or more of the following consequences:

1. **Low self-worth:** We won't like ourselves.

2. **Lack of self-confidence:** We feel unable to change our life situations.

3. **Depression:** We store up anger and pain and get sick over it.

4. **Psychosomatic illnesses:** Our repressed feelings and low self-worth actually create high blood pressure, ulcers, and lower the body's immune responses.

5. **Unhealthy relationships:** We try to "swallow up" and control others, or vice versa. Inappropriate sexual behavior is also an example of this.

6. **Co-dependency:** We focus so much on another person that we lose ourselves. This is also called people-addiction.

7. **Other addictions:** Predilections to alcohol/drugs, food, work, sex, gambling, shopping, television, video games, and so forth, might result from the "black hole" inside of us left by our emotional and spiritual bankruptcy.

These are all terrible consequences, and countless people in our world are experiencing them as a way of life. The reason for this, as we have already mentioned, is that most of us did not adequately learn the necessary relationship skills which serve to "inoculate" us from emotional/spiritual diseases. More than likely, our parents and teachers did not know these skills so it would have been impossible for them to teach us. Typically, our parents, teachers, and ministers have focused on values, "shoulds," and "shouldn'ts" in nurturing human character. While there is no denying the importance of ethical guidance, this does not satisfy our emotional and spiritual hungers.

In many ways, then, most of us — adults and children alike — find it necessary to be "returning to school," as it were, to receive "remedial instruction" concerning relationship skills. If we are lucky, we can find this instruction in our religious affiliations. Quite frequently, however, it will be through a counseling program or a personal growth series of some kind that we pick up these skills. Obviously, too, there are many books which can help us to grow.

TEACHING RELATIONSHIP SKILLS

If we were to teach a course on intrapersonal and interpersonal intelligence, what would we teach? This is the question to be answered in this book. It is an attempt to identify specific skills which help to bring out the innate relational intelligence in all of us. Just as an English teacher (who is instructing pupils for the development of linguistic intelligence) finds it necessary to teach the rules of grammar, so, too, there are essential skills which must be learned if we are to grow in the relational intelligences.

If we learn a skill and practice it, there is a strong likelihood that it will then become a habit. Consider driving a car, for example. When we first begin driving, there is a heightened sense of consciousness about everything. We think: "Am I giving it enough gas? Where's that signal light now? Am I too close to that other car?" Gradually we learn the skills necessary to drive a car safely, and the unconscious appropriates these skills so that we do not have to think about them so self-consciously. Seasoned drivers do not think about giving the car enough gas or using the turn signal: They just do these things as a matter of course. How wonderful it would be if, similarly, we would train ourselves to foster such habits as emotional awareness, listening, validating, and the surrender of faith! There are many of us who can do that; but, as is the case with reading, writing, adding, subtracting, and driving a car, we must first go through a period of uncertainty and self-consciousness before the skills become part of our normal patterns of behaving.

The skills discussed in this book cannot be mastered as a result of a single reading. The first time through might seem awkward, but practicing them will eventually produce healthy habits of relating. Also, we need to admit that we are never finished growing in relationships; as we grow and change, these skills must be applied in the ever-new situations in which we find ourselves.

A special distinction needs to be made between skills and gifts. Some persons may not be very gifted in spatial intelligence — they may not be able to draw, for example. However, they may love to express themselves in speaking and writing and they develop this gift by the practice of linguistic skills. This is true of the practical and mystical intelligences as well. Relationship skills can help to deepen our experiences of love of self, neighbor, and God, but the skills do not of themselves produce love. Love is a gift that comes to us in mystery, and we should not lose sight of this lest we think we can earn love or feel loving whenever we wish. Rather, relationship skills give love a chance to happen within and among us.

How To Use This Book

These pages include a formal and straightforward presentation of the basic intrapersonal and interpersonal skills. Our everyday relationships require the use of a combination of skills at any moment; but if we are to grow we must emphasize the importance of identifying specific skills and working on them. In doing so, we do not mean to neglect the other skills. If, for example, we are working this week on learning to identify our feelings, it does not follow that we are neglecting our need to listen. Indeed, the more intensely we work on one specific skill, the more likely it will be that we shall recognize opportunities to exercise other skill areas as well.

This book has been written in such a manner that it can be used as a text for the readers' personal growth, and/or for use by parents, teachers, ministers, counselors, and others in a position to teach relationship skills. Because a necessary part of skill development is practice, each chapter will include certain "homework assignments" for individual use and for use by relationship teachers.

Readers are strongly encouraged to do these assignments if growth in relationship skills is desired. People do not learn to play a piano by simply reading a book about it. Likewise, simply reading about relationship skills will be of limited value without practicing them. "To know, and not to do, is not yet to know," states an Eastern maxim.

So, if readers want a book on personal growth, they have one here; but it is hoped that all will do some of the homework, too. If they feel the assignment is too easy, or if they believe they have already mastered the skill in question, then they should make up their own tougher assignment, or move ahead.

There are two parts to this work: one treats intrapersonal skills (relating with yourself); the other treats interpersonal skills (relating with others). In real life, all human intelligences are inter-related; no intelligence is nurtured in complete isolation from the rest. For example, intrapersonal skills are first learned in the context of interpersonal relationships. Later, mystical intelligence complements both. Nevertheless, there are different skills which must be learned for these relationship intelligences — hence, the two parts of this book.

Readers will be asked to do daily practices at the end of each chapter. One of these practices is journaling — a powerful way to get in touch with the inner life. Simply thinking out the homework assignments is not enough. There is something about journaling that relaxes the mind, opening it up to its inner depths. Finally, journaling provides a record of growth in relational intelligence.

It was to provide a comprehensive reference for my own work-shop on relationship skills that I first wrote the lecture notes and activities which I am now presenting in book form. In the past I had found it necessary to recommend three or four books for each of the relational intelligences. This proved to be a positive hindrance to participants who did not read very much. I also found it necessary to create experiential activities to help participants practice these skills, for most of the books offered no such opportunities. This material has been piloted in workshops and short courses with adults and youth groups and has been most favorably evaluated.

Here are some recommended ways of using this book:

1. As a self-help guide for personal growth in relationships.

2. As a text on relationships for high school and college students.

3. As a resource book for parents, teachers, and counselors.

4. As a vehicle for workshops and support groups concerned with growth in relationships.

My hope and my prayer is that *Lessons in Loving* will help to promote a serious approach to growth in relational intelligence. If this work makes but a small contribution toward that goal, I will be satisfied.

Philip St. Romain

PART ONE

INTRAPERSONAL INTELLIGENCE: RELATING WITH YOURSELF

"Of all the people you'll ever know, you're the only one who will never leave you." This saying underscores the importance of intrapersonal intelligence, or relating with yourself.

Intrapersonal intelligence is defined as the capacity to discriminate among one's feelings and, eventually, to label them and understand their relation to other psychic processes. Other terms often used to describe this intelligence are self-esteem and self-discipline. Neither of these terms is completely synonymous with intrapersonal intelligence, however. In fact, they are constituents and consequences of intrapersonal intelligence. Self-knowledge and the ability to nurture yourself are closer to the point. Knowing how your mind works and how to live with your mind is a working definition that could also be used.

Intrapersonal intelligence begins to emerge at a very early age and continues to grow throughout life. Although your learning potential changes through the years, you must nonetheless employ the same core intrapersonal skills in the ongoing integration of your life experiences. This integration is greatly enhanced by your growth in the other intelligences. Your growth in spirituality gives you a larger context in which to situate your life experiences;

growth in language skills equips you with new words for identifying, defining, and shaping your experiences. As you grow in your own self-understanding, your relationships with others change, too. In fact, without a healthy growth in intrapersonal skills, it will be impossible to enjoy interpersonal relationships.

Growing in intrapersonal intelligence does not come easily. Unlike many other self-help books, this book will not promise fulfillment, beauty, prosperity, and happiness to those who practice intrapersonal skills. Growth in intrapersonal intelligence will sometimes be painful, for it will lead you to face certain truths about yourself that you have been repressing. Although the gentlest approach possible is presented here, it goes without saying that you should work at your own pace. If you persist in the struggle, you will grow each day in a fuller experience of the fruits of intrapersonal intelligence: self-worth, self-discipline, and the freedom to choose your own way in life. Obviously these outcomes are worth the struggle to attain them.

1

NAME YOUR FEELINGS

You could begin your examination of intrapersonal skills in a number of places: your dreams, hopes, self-perceptions, and so forth. Emotional awareness will be the starting point here because how you feel about yourself and life is a never-ending human preoccupation. Seldom do you persist in doing things that make you feel bad if you can help it. To the contrary, you generally pursue activities and relationships that make you feel better.

Another reason for beginning with emotional awareness is because feelings reveal the meaning of the events of life. Think about that for a moment. When people tell you they're sad, what's the first question that comes to your mind? You want to know why they're sad, of course. Feelings are like spiritual barometers, or windows into the soul. By becoming aware of your feelings you can then begin to examine the underlying perceptions and beliefs which give rise to them.

Feelings are the ''energy stuff'' of relationships, and growing in relationships is what this book is all about. It is possible to be connected with other people through the medium of ideas, or shared activities. But it is not until you are also emotionally connected that the relationship can be considered meaningful. Connecting emotionally with others presupposes your ability to manage your own emotional life.

The most obvious reason so many relationships fail today is because people quit feeling close and affectionate toward one another. You would not want to stay in a relationship where you feel almost nothing positive, or maybe a whole lot of negatives, or, most tragically, maybe nothing at all. It is true that affectionate feelings do not constitute the essence of love, but they do help to keep things going. If you don't frequently feel warm and close toward another person, then maybe there is no love at all. Although you can do almost nothing about the emotional life of others, you do have much control on your side of the relationship. Sometimes the changes you make for yourself will provide the stimulus needed to rejuvenate an arid relationship.

KINDS OF FEELINGS

There are four major groups of feelings: glad, sad, mad, and scared. Within each group are various shades of feelings. For example, within the "mad" category, anger, aggravation, indignation, fury, rage, and hatred can be identified. These are all mad feelings, but they describe very different experiences. Glad feelings include such states as joy, pleasure, comfort, elation, euphoria, and satisfaction. These, too, describe different experiences. Emotional awareness calls for becoming more conscious of the subtle shades of feelings that accompany your life experiences.

Paying attention to your body is one way to get in touch with your feelings. Several old aphorisms have long noted the body-feeling connections. Consider, for example, the following:

"She makes me sick to my stomach!"

"He was so angry he was pulling his hair out!"

"I laughed till I cried!"

"I was so worried I couldn't sleep."

"He's a real pain in the neck!"

Your body is very responsive to your emotional states. As the above sayings indicate, nausea, hair-pulling, weeping, insomnia, as well as neck and back pains are often the result of feelings. So are fidgety legs and hands (anxiety), certain skin rashes (repressed fear), clenched fists (anger), folded arms (shyness), grinding teeth (resentment), and many others. Entire books have been written about just this one small part of intrapersonal intelligence! Learn everything you can about your feelings from your body, for unexpressed feelings still reside in your bodily tissues.

IMPORTANCE OF EMOTIONAL AWARENESS

Emotional awareness is possible only in the present moment. It is often profitable to get in touch with past emotional states, and it is good to allay anxieties about the future by planning ahead. But most people live too much of their lives with their attention gazing backward in guilt and regret, or forward in worry and self-concern. Present-moment living means living in the now, where real life is happening to you. Learning to be aware of your feelings in a now-moment is an excellent way to surrender more deeply to the process of growth that is taking place in your life.

Many people (maybe most?) do not have a high degree of emotional awareness. Stresses from everyday life and from watching too much TV make for emotional illiterates. If you have chosen this lifestyle, you can change it if you wish. Nobody makes you watch TV, and your attitude about school or job is yours to change, too.

DAILY PRACTICES

1. Ask yourself through the day, ''What am I feeling right now?'' Try to be as specific as possible. Do this often enough and it will become a habit.

2. When you get in touch with uncomfortable feelings, do not judge yourself because of these feelings. Feelings in themselves are neither good nor bad. Simply accept yourself and your feelings as you are.

3. Reduce or eliminate altogether the time you spend watching TV or listening to the radio. TV and radio overwhelm consciousness with an array of perceptions no one can sufficiently process. The result is emotional numbness.

4. If you find it difficult to get in touch with your feelings, start keeping a ''Journal of Feelings.'' Using a notebook, draw a

line down the page. Use one page for each day. Take notes as illustrated below. Be honest with yourself.

What Happened Today	How I Felt
Up late, hurrying out of house to get to work; traffic jam.	Angry, nervous, afraid to face boss.
Worked on Jones account with Sally all morning.	Peaceful, cheerful, with few irritations.

5. In a similar exercise, reverse the columns and reflect on times you experience your predominant feelings about your family members, friends, job/school, Church, God, and so forth.

Person/ Group	Predominant Feelings	Times When I Feel This Way
My Spouse	Gratitude	When she cooks a special meal. When she affirms my care for our kids. When she prays with me.
	Anger	When I'm tired and she asks me to run errands. When she interrupts me while I'm talking to her.

2

RECOGNIZE THE WAYS YOU EXPRESS FEELINGS

Feelings are a form of psychic energy. Whenever you have a feeling, you channel its energy in one of four ways:

1. **By ignoring or repressing it directly:** You deny the feeling by smothering it; the energy then moves into the unconscious mind. If you do this too often, the energy is forced into the body, where it is stored in the tissues.

2. **By acting it out openly:** You do what the feeling makes you feel like doing. If you are angry, you yell and scream — maybe even hit someone or throw things around. If you are happy, you smile or giggle or simply beam; if you are sad, you cry. Acting out discharges emotional energy, but sometimes it gets you into other troubles.

3. **By displaying your feelings indirectly:** You use sarcasm, place the blame on others, or lecture others when you're angry (this is called a ''you message''); you laugh when you're really scared or embarrassed (this is called incongruency); you take your feelings out on someone or something else (this is called displacement). Here the emotional energy is released, but people may be repelled in the process or else confused about what you're really feeling.

4. **By expressing your feelings openly:** By means of "I messages" you simply state what you feel and the circumstances that provoked your feelings without blaming or judging others. Examples of this would be: "When you hug me, I feel happy," or "I feel angry and defensive when you yell at me." These espressions are infinitely preferable to "You make me mad," or even, "You make me happy." They enable you to take ownership of your feelings and to express them in a respectful manner. "I messages" also leave others free to adjust their behavior in such a manner as to meet your needs.

CONSEQUENCES OF EMOTIONAL EXPRESSION

Quite obviously, each of the four methods of expressing feelings carries with it consequences relative to your relationships. How you express anger is especially important. For example, suppose you are upset with your wife because she forgot to pick up a package for you on her way home from work. If you repress your anger, this will leave you feeling cold and distant toward her; doubtless, she'll sense something is wrong, but she will wonder what it is. If you yell and scream, you'll feel better for a while (then you'll probably feel guilty), but she'll feel worse (and, in fact, she may be glad she forgot that wretched package). If you use sarcasm — "Guess you had more important things to think about than me, right?" — or some other such words, the gulf between the two of you will widen. But if you simply say (and say it with feeling), "I feel angry because you forgot to get my package," you are taking care of your need to express your anger, and you have a better chance of getting a hearing from your wife. She may even apologize for her mistake. In such circumstances, an apology from her would help to diminish your anger so that the two of you could then get down to the real issue: forgetting the package. When you deny your true feelings by yelling, using sarcasm, or blaming others, you are adding new issues. The real concern here is your wife's damaged ego.

No doubt many potentially good relationships are lost each year simply because people do not express their feelings in appropriate ways. For example, people may add issue upon issue, compounding the very real problems that life presents to them each day until, after a while, they do not even like the other person anymore. (Hurt and disappointment turn to anger; repressed anger to resentment; resentment to indifference — and, without counseling, this is the end.)

In a spiritual context, you can see how the manner in which you express your feelings brings you closer together (a movement of grace) or separates you (a sinful situation). That is why this second intrapersonal skill is so important. The message here is this: Be aware of the four ways in which you express your feelings and recognize the consequences to relationships that come with each.

FOUR SPECIAL PROBLEMS

Some people have great difficulty identifying their feelings because they automatically repress them. This can occur in your life if you have grown up in a home where your feelings have been discounted and invalidated. Here are four different ways this can happen:

1. When other people say, "You shouldn't feel that way." The message you pick up (especially as a child) is that it's not OK to have *that* feeling (even if that's not what the other person wanted you to perceive).

2. When you believe that it is wrong to have certain feelings. For example, you learned that it was a violation of the Fourth Commandment to be angry toward your parents. Being a fairly normal child, you often became angry at your parents, but you repressed these feelings and later took them out on others and yourself.

3. When you are taught such nonsense as "Big boys don't cry." This gives the message: "Crying is not OK. You have to express this feeling in another way." An idiotic song which was popular for a while has the refrain: "Don't cry out loud: just keep it inside, learn how to hide your feelings."

4. When you grow up in a home where parents seldom talk about feelings and seldom take time to listen to your feelings. "People don't feel" is the message here.

Because the above four situations are fairly common in most homes, schools, and Churches, many people have learned to smother their feelings. Such people often say, "I don't have any feelings," or "I feel numb," or "I'm an introverted thinker." But the truth is that all persons (even introverted thinkers) have a multitude of feelings every day. They don't feel them because they have trained themselves not to; such repression is actually a way they express feelings unconsciously.

This learned habit of repressing feelings can make you susceptible to a variety of psychosomatic illnesses and addictions. It also sets you up for the "stuff-and-explode" cycle. This happens when you repress and repress until you can't stand it any longer; then you explode — act out — the sum total of these feelings. The clinical name for this is augmentation. As mentioned above, there are many consequences in your relationships which ensue from repressing feelings, which eventually surface in the emotional abuse of others through "you messages" and the "acting out" process.

The good news is that you can learn to express your feelings in appropriate ways. The bad news, however, is that you might first have to unlearn some other ways of acting.

DAILY PRACTICES

1. As you strive to become more aware of your feelings through the day, say to yourself: "Right now I'm feeling . . . (name the emotion). What am I going to do with this feeling? Which of the four ways is the most loving way to express it?"

2. Add a column entitled "How I expressed it" to your journal of feelings explained at the end of Chapter One. Here you identify which of the four ways you used to express your feelings and how this affected you and others.

3

EXAMINE YOUR DEFENSIVE BEHAVIOR

How many times have you heard other people justify their behavior in terms of the external circumstances that provoked them? Two children fighting might say: "He hit me so I hit him back," or "She called me a name so I hit her." Adults are often no better. "Everybody's doing it!" is their excuse for irresponsible behavior. The assumption here seems to be that a certain course of behavior is automatically provoked by a certain situation. When caught in a traffic jam, some people get angry and scream and yell and honk their horns. When asked why they do these things, they say: "Can't you see there's a traffic jam?"

Growth in intrapersonal intelligence requires that you recognize the fact that you are responsible for your own feelings and how you express them. It's a choice between acting and reacting. When you react, you give other people, places, and things power over your behavior. ("You make me so mad!") Reacting means acting out of conditioning — like an animal that has been trained to behave in a certain way when the right cues are given. But you, as human beings, are capable of breaking free from your reactive, conditioned behavior (if you want to). It is in your power to act and not just to react! You may choose to behave in a different manner than your conditioning has led you in the past; you may also choose to go with the old behavior, in which case you will not be merely reacting. *The important thing is that you learn to choose your behavioral alternative and not let external events run your life.*

DEFENSES AND REACTIONS

Most people have been conditioned to behave in certain ways when they experience certain feelings. Their most common form of emotional expression is to smother their feelings and make use of "you messages." If they don't learn another way, then this is what they will continue to do.

One of the primary obstacles to a change in the way you express your feelings is the system of defenses which you have erected to protect yourself through the years. A defense may be defined as any behavior which serves to protect your self-concept. This in itself is not bad, for you need to learn to set boundaries for yourself. The problem is that your defenses may be too rigid. This happens when you have a poor self-concept and are filled with emotional pain. In such a state, defenses keep you locked into selfish ego states and, consequently, incapable of meeting your emotional needs. Your loneliness and bitterness then increase, and this fortifies your defensiveness and locks you into the addictive process.

To show how this works, consider the case of Mary, who is a perfectionist with regard to her work. For Mary, anything less than total perfection and absolute approval by others is generally unsatisfactory. Furthermore, her belief is such that if anyone catches her at a mistake, it means that she is a "bad" person. She learned this from her parents through many years of abusive discipline, and so now she takes this attitude with her wherever she goes. Whenever her family and co-workers say anything which in any way indicates to her that she is imperfect, her feelings become hurt. What she does with these hurt feelings, however, is to bombard people with "you messages," then minimize her behavior and give herself excuses as to why she blundered. Sometimes she even denies her mistakes, which is just plain dishonesty.

DEFENSIVENESS AND SELF-WORTH

A healthy sense of inner security does not rest on the basis of being well-defended, but on the awareness that you are loved no matter what you do. If you are fortunate, this sense of being so loved will come from your human relationships. More than likely, however, other people have loved you conditionally — with strings attached. Therefore you must make a decision to love yourself regardless of how other people have treated you. For many, the belief that God always loves you just as you are is the basis of this self-love. It is here that you discover the linkage between religious faith and intrapersonal intelligence.

Self-love may not come easily for you. You may have a survivor's mentality, distrusting other people and basing your security on your ability to put up a good defense. As mentioned earlier, this attitude only results in more loneliness and defensiveness. There must be another way out.

And there is! Even though you may still be struggling with faith, it is possible to admit that defensiveness is counterproductive. When you get right down to it, what is there to defend anyway — the self-concept?

Look at it this way: if your self-concept requires defensiveness and dishonesty to sustain it, then it is an unhealthy self-concept, and you need to change it for the sake of your own happiness.

Also consider this: If you have even a slightly healthy self-concept, other people cannot significantly hurt you. If their criticism is harsh and inappropriate, you do not have to accept what they say as your truth, and you can express your feelings to get relief. If, on the other hand, the feedback of others is true, then perhaps you can learn something about yourself that will help you grow. In either case, you do not have to lose self-worth.

Dishonest and inappropriate defenses are among the primary obstacles to personal growth. Letting down your guard is often difficult, but it is possible if you are willing to work at it.

The first step is to become aware of when you are getting defensive. Simply admit what you are feeling and how your defenses are arising. If you can do this, you can actually make a decision to drop your defenses to listen to the other. Your "self-talk" might proceed in this manner: "I'm really angry about what this person is saying right now, and I'm wanting to minimize, blame, and attack him/her for it. But what is being said cannot really hurt me because I'm loved no matter what. In fact, maybe I can learn something from this. I will listen." Then, if you wish you may add a prayer for the grace of being able to listen and love to the end of this self-talk. This turns the tables completely, moving you from an attitude of fearful defensiveness to a willingness to love and grow.

SPECIAL PROBLEMS

It is a fact, of course, that many people live in abusive situations where it would be foolish to let down their defenses. Children of alcoholics, for example, have taken on defenses as a matter of emotional survival. For such children (and others who live in turmoil), it is important to find a safe place where they can learn to talk and listen without being defensive. If they do not learn to do this when they are young, this will become their suit of armor wherever they go as adults.

A suit of armor is handy in time of war, but a nuisance when it's time for hugging. The problem for many is that they may not even know how to remove this armor. This is where the Adult Children of Alcoholics group can help. This and other support groups and therapies for anyone with a poor self-concept and a rigid system of defenses are highly recommended.

DAILY PRACTICES

1. Give an example of a time when you have used one of the defenses described in this chapter. (For additional insight, ask someone you trust to read what you have written in order to give you feedback about your defensiveness.)

2. For each of the defenses listed in the chart on the following page, indicate whether you utilize it Never (N), Seldom (S), Often (O), or Frequently (F). In your journal write an example of a time you have used this defense. (For additional insight, ask someone you trust to use this exercise to give you feedback about your defensiveness.)

N	S	O	F	Type of Defensive Behavior
				1. Denying: "No. That's not the way it happened."
				2. Minimizing: "It's not that bad!"
				3. Explaining: Giving background, details.
				4. Justifying: Giving yourself reasons.
				5. Remaining silent: Not responding.
				6. Counterattacking: Bringing up other's faults.
				7. Using sarcasm: "I suppose you're perfect!"
				8. Agreeing: "Yeh. Uh-huh. You're right."
				9. Joking: Using humor inappropriately. Making light of the matter.
				10. Blaming: Nonacceptance of personal responsibility.
				11. Changing the subject: Closing off the issue prematurely.
				12. Trivializing: Picking out one little detail that's not quite right and discussing that rather than the larger issues and feelings.

4

UNDERSTAND YOUR FEELINGS

Feelings refer to the pleasurable or painful sensations you experience when you are stirred to sympathy, anger, fear, love, grief, and so on. Of themselves they are neither good nor bad, and you should learn to use them properly. For example, if you — as a parent — feel anger toward your children, you should admit it to yourself rather than repress it "because a loving parent must never get angry with the children." This simple acceptance of self as a feeling person may not come easily because you have been taught that some feelings are not OK.

This notion about the moral neutrality of feelings is more clearly understood today, thanks to the facts revealed by the behavioral sciences. Morality has to do with behavior and with beliefs. When people say, "You shouldn't feel that way," they are attaching moral judgment to a feeling, and this is inappropriate. What is usually meant when this is said is this, "I don't think you see it clearly, for if you did, you wouldn't feel that way." Unfortunately, the message that comes across is "It is wrong to have that feeling."

If, then, feelings are neither good nor bad, does that mean you cannot understand why you feel the way you do? Not at all! There *is* usually a reason why you feel the way you feel, and it is important that you understand the roots of your feelings. In short: *You do not just feel, you feel because . . .*

Six Common Feelings

Listed below are a few general statements about your most common feelings:

1. You feel *angry* when your wants/needs are not met. You are usually *hurt* and *disappointed* when this happens. Anger, then, is usually a secondary feeling, with hurt, disappointment, and fear being the primary feelings. You are "angry with" your hurt, disappointment, and fear.

2. You feel *sad* when you suffer the loss of an important person, position, or thing.

3. You feel *glad* when your wants/needs are met.

4. You feel *guilty* when you behave in a manner that conflicts with your values.

5. You feel *scared* when you have a problem that threatens the fulfillment of your wants/needs, but you have no solution to this problem.

6. You feel *shame* when you sense that you are no good or act as if you're no good.

Note that all of the above statements have to do with how you view yourself, your needs, and your values — all of which belong to the life of the mind. This is not to deny the role of physical health and sickness in your emotional life, however. If you are sick, then it is likely that your feelings will be depressed, sad, or flat. Similarly, certain biochemical fluctuations can produce mood swings within you. Research has shown that nutrition affects your feelings, and, of course, mood-altering drugs change the way you feel about things. While focusing on intrapersonal intelligence, the concern of this part of the book will be with feelings and their relation to other psychic processes.

A CASE OF ANGER

Much can be learned from experience of just one feeling — anger, for instance. In accord with what was written above, you experience anger when your wants/needs are not met. When you feel angry, then, the issue you must deal with is this: "What are the wants/needs of mine that are not being met?" The "I message" can help you get in touch with those wants/needs. "I feel angry about (*this*) because of (*that*)" you tell yourself in the "I message." The *because of* part of the message helps you get in touch with those wants/needs that are not being met.

To exemplify, consider the husband who sometimes gets angry when the house is a mess — which is especially likely to happen when he's augmenting from other feelings. He then tells his family: "I feel angry about this dirty, cluttered-up house of ours because I'd like to relax now, and all I see is work needing to be done." (Other common reasons are: "We have company coming" or "You haven't done your chores.") His wants/needs are relaxation, and he'd like a bit of physical order to help him to do that. In truth, he is really disappointed about all this. If he can get past his anger and talk about his disappointment, he will get more emotional relief.

This same husband provides a further example. When his wife was pregnant, she would become tired and nauseated during the first trimester. At that time he often became angry because she showed so little affection toward him. She also let her chores slide, which meant that he had to do more (and he was already pushed to his limits). The "I message" was this: "I feel angry about this because I have to do my work and yours too — with little affectionate compensation from you, I might add." He felt guilt about this anger for a while. "How can I be upset about someone in her condition?" he'd ask himself. Nevertheless, angry he was and repression only increased the anger within him, leading to coldness and resentment. His wants/needs for affection, appreciation, and practical help with the housework and children were not being met, and he was angry. In truth, he was also lonely, hurting, and depressed, but he had to get past his anger to experience those deeper layers of feeling.

Obviously, the wants/needs of the above-mentioned husband are sometimes pretty unreasonable. The purpose of this book, then, is to explore ways to change those types of wants/needs, values, and perceptions so that they conform more favorably with the ways of love. The main point for now is to acknowledge that your feelings have much to tell you about who you are right now: what your beliefs, values, and expectations are about. Feelings do not lie! As such, they are open windows into the soul.

DAILY PRACTICES

1. Spend some time reflecting on the reasons why in the recent past you have felt angry, guilty, sad, glad, afraid, and ashamed. One good way would be to build on your work from pages 17-18 and 22. Use the reasons given in points 1-6 in this chapter. A suggested approach is listed below:

Feelings and Experiences	Reasons I Feel This Way
I felt *angry* about . . .	*because*
	(wants/needs not being met)
— the dirty house	— I was tired; I needed order.
— breakfast not being cooked on time	— I was hungry and running late.
— being caught in a traffic jam	— I wanted to get home.
I feel *guilty* about . . .	*because*
	(behavior conflict values)
— yelling at the children	— I didn't show patience.
— spreading ugly rumors	— it hurts another's reputation.

5

ANALYZE YOUR ACTIONS

In his book, *The Christian Vision,* (Tabor Publishing, 1984), Father John Powell tells the following story. A man comes home drunk one night, only to observe a thirty-five-foot snake on his lawn. He becomes afraid so he gets a hoe and chops it up. The next morning he discovers, to his immense humiliation, that he has chopped his garden hose into pieces.

This story serves well to illustrate the dynamics of human behavior. The beginning of behavior is perception. The thoughts, feelings, decisions, and actions follow from perceptions. If you see a hose as a snake, then — to you — it is a snake. That alcohol and drugs can alter your perception is another point to be considered.

Now note that the perception of the snake produced fear. Why is this? The simple presence of a snake is not an adequate explanation for fear, is it? Seeing something you do not expect to see will always produce a temporary shock, or surprise. Afterward, you come to your wits and begin to analyze the situation. More than likely, the man in the story believed that the snake was dangerous, and that it posed a threat to himself and his children. *That* is what produced the fear. But what if, instead of being afraid of snakes, he liked snakes? He might have thought: "Hmmm, that's a pretty big snake, but it's not one of the poisonous kind. What a great pet it would make for the children!" With such thoughts in mind, he might even feel excitement and delight about the presence of the snake.

Next comes the chopping. You've probably already guessed that he was simply acting out his fear. "Of course I chopped it up: it was a snake — a snake, dummy!" he would explain. Even given the fact of his fear, however, he had other alternatives besides killing the poor thing. He might have just left it alone, hoping that it would slither away during the night; he also might have called the police to come and get it (but they would have noted his intoxicated condition).

In short, given the perception of a snake (even one that's really a hose), there are numerous ways of thinking, feeling, and behaving toward the snake. Between the stimulus — snake — and the response — chopping — there's a lot of mental ground to cover. Growing in intrapersonal intelligence will help you become more familiar with that ground.

ROLE OF CONSCIOUSNESS

The model used to explain the dynamics of human behavior is outlined below. Like all models or maps, it doesn't explain everything. But it can help you find your way around the psyche, and that's why it is presented here.

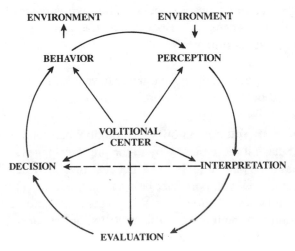

NOTE: Most decisions are made after the interpreted perceptions have been evaluated by way of the feelings; however, some will be made on a strictly rational basis — with no reference to feelings whatsoever.

33

The meaning of the terms used in the above model are defined below.

1. **Volitional Center of Consciousness:** This is the seat of personal, subjective awareness and desire. (It is in this state that you perceive, interpret, evaluate, and decide.)

2. **Perception:** Here you receive data from your senses, intuition, imagination, memory, or awareness of need. (You can have perception about almost anything that goes on outside and inside of you.)

3. **Interpretation:** Here you examine the perceived data in light of your beliefs (the thought patterns that you have committed to memory) and your values (those beliefs that enable you to meet your basic needs/wants).

4. **Evaluation:** Here you weigh the perceived and interpreted data in light of the feelings by which you express the meaning you attach to your beliefs and values. (Although intimately related to beliefs, feelings are a form of psychic activity in their own right.)

5. **Decision:** Here you determine what you are going to do about what is going on in your consciousness. (This step is reactive and responsive to the process described above. It is a conscious, reflective, deliberate action.)

6. **Behavior:** Here you act out the decision you have just made. (It can be expressed outwardly or inwardly or both.)

So there you have it: You now know why you do what you do. This, too, should make it more clear why in the previous pages so much attention has been paid to feelings — because they provide a key to understanding how you perceive, believe, and behave. The man in the snake story was aware of two things: the snake and his fear. The perception and the feeling came almost simultaneously, even though the perception was filtered through his belief system.

Whether you realize it or not, you are often like him, aware of your job and your boredom, or a traffic jam and your anger, or any other event. What you must begin to do is to see the other processes which contribute to your feelings.

ROLE OF THE UNCONSCIOUS

It should be mentioned here that there are unconscious dimensions to your perceptions, beliefs, feelings, and desires. Although many writers believe that much attention should be devoted to the study of the unconscious, this writer does not see it as an important part of intrapersonal intelligence. After all, the unconscious is, by definition, something you do not know consciously, and if you cannot be conscious of it, then you cannot deal with it head on.

All that is really necessary here is to have an open and friendly attitude toward the unconscious dimensions of the mind. If the unconscious has any message to communicate, it will surface into consciousness through intuition, dreams, or projected feelings. When unconscious energies become conscious, they can be dealt with as with other data.

DAILY PRACTICES

1. Think about this statement: "It's not so much what happens to me that causes me to feel a certain way; it's what I tell myself about what happens to me." Do you agree with this? Why or why not?

2. Take a look at the reasons for your feelings discovered in the journal exercises outlined at the end of Chapter One. What can you learn about your beliefs? Are there beliefs you would like to change? Later chapters will propose a process for changing unreasonable beliefs. For now, simply get in touch with a few of your previous beliefs.

6

Reexamine Your Beliefs

Years ago, most husbands expected their wives to cook, keep house, take care of the children, and stay at home. But many husbands today have changed their way of thinking in these areas. They now share responsibilities with their wives. This transition has not always come about smoothly and without incident. There may have been many nasty little scenes along the way, but it seems that the majority of men have now adjusted to the "liberated" woman.

The above situation and the warning of many fine counselors points out this fact: Change is possible, but it always requires giving up something to make way for something new. Chapter Four discussed the reasons why you feel the way you feel. The role of consciousness treated in Chapter Five demonstrated that your feelings derive from your perceptions and beliefs. Feelings, then, can help you to get in touch with what beliefs you have had programmed into you through the years. Getting in touch with these beliefs is very important, for your beliefs guide and control your lives. No doubt you are quite happy with some of your beliefs but miserable about others.

Feelings and Beliefs

The best way to get in touch with your beliefs is by paying attention to your feelings. As has been previously stated, most feelings spring from your wants/needs — whether they are met (pleasure), or not met (anger), or threatened (fear), and so forth. When you experience any feeling, you can learn much about yourself by noting your responses to these two questions:

"Why do I feel the way I do? (The answer lies in the three-part "I message"): I feel (this or these emotions) about (name the circumstance or behavior) because (of the following expectations)."

"Are my expectations and beliefs (which are found in the "because" part of the "I message") reasonable?

It takes great courage to ask these two questions. It takes even more humility to admit, in response to the second one, that your expectations and beliefs are sometimes unreasonable and un loving, and so ought to be changed. Because of hurt pride and the habit of doing things a certain way, it would be a nuisance to change. Paying attention to yourself and asking the two questions above takes some work, the result of which may not be pleasant at all! It is much easier to live "spontaneously" (meaning, here, reactively and unreflectively) and to blame your boredom and ennui on the people around you or society in general. This won't make you happy, however.

As an example of this process, suppose you (a husband) are angry because your wife hasn't kept the house in order. Here's the "I message": "I feel angry about this dirty house because my wife has not cleaned it." (This is in response to the first question.)

Now for the second question: "Is it reasonable for me to expect that my wife should have cleaned the house?" Maybe it is. Maybe you have agreed-upon chores, and one of hers was to clean the house. But maybe — just maybe — this expectation was not arrived at through conscious, loving negotiation. A good number of husbands have discovered that they had lots of expectations about men and women's roles that were based upon what they had been taught in the home, Church, and school.

FORM HEALTHY BELIEFS

"What makes a belief unreasonable?" "How can I know whether my beliefs need to be changed?" These are very good questions — among the best that can be asked.

In response, it can be said that some beliefs and expectations are situationally determined, and so must be constantly negotiated with others. For example, it is reasonable for a father to expect his children to be able to do more to help out around the house as they grow older; it is unreasonable for him to expect that his wife can help out very much when she is sick. If he does not change his expectations to suit the new situation, he will probably become angry and unyielding.

In addition to situational factors, however, the reasonableness of your own personal beliefs derives from their grounding in truth and their potential for love or abuse. This means that you will also need to consult your religious and philosophical beliefs about reality to decide whether what you believe is true and good. For example, in deciding what is reasonable and loving about a belief, you should consider the life and teachings of Christ. Because you are Christian and are trying to adopt a Christian vision of reality, you find it very helpful to focus on Christ in forming healthy beliefs. Those who are not Christians will have to decide upon what basis they will accept or reject certain beliefs.

So here is very good news indeed! You can change your feelings by changing your beliefs and the expectations they generate. It is not so much what happens to you that determines the way you feel, but what you tell yourself about what happens to you. If you, by chance, get angry very often, something can be done about it. By changing many of the rigid expectations of yourself and others, and by accepting the things you cannot change, you can practically eliminate anger from your life. This in itself is a great liberation!

DAILY PRACTICES

A number of life-limiting beliefs are listed on the following pages. To the extent that these beliefs are unconscious, they will distort your vision and contaminate your feelings. This survey is intended to help you determine the strength or weakness of each belief within you. By doing this you will be able to identify beliefs you need to change. For help in this area, consult Chapter Five for insights into your beliefs.

1. **Self-righteous Pride:** Based on a sense of superiority, it leads to condescension, anger, judgmentalism, factions, loneliness. It often derives from bigoted parenting. Such a person is practically saying:

   - People having hard times probably deserve it.
   - Other people's problems give me a sense of how smart I really am.
   - Other people can't teach me anything unless they're smarter than I am.
   - My sex is superior to the other.
   - The people of my race are superior to others.
   - Younger or older people can't do anything as well as my age group.
   - My beliefs are absolutely true; if you disagree with me, you are wrong.
   - Mature people must never cry nor show any emotional distress.
   - My self-worth is best measured by my competitive edge over others.

Intensity

(Weak)			(Strong)	
1	2	3	4	5

2. **Guilt-ridden Pride:** Built on reluctance to face wrongs done, it resists the need to seek forgiveness. It often derives from autocratic and punitive parenting styles and thus leads to shame. Such a person is practically saying:

   - To apologize when I do wrong is to give in to another and is a sign of weakness.
   - It's not my fault when I do wrong; it's usually the other's.

Intensity

(Weak)			(Strong)	
1	2	3	4	5

- God can't forgive me, I'm too . . .
- It's OK to do wrong, just so long as I don't get caught.
- My sins don't hurt anyone but me.
- I've done some really terrible things for which I cannot be forgiven.

3. **Ambitious Pride:** This leads to an exaggerated sense of responsibility, insufficient recreation, and emotional burnout. It often derives from perfectionistic expectations by parents, teachers, and ministers. Such a person is practically saying:

- I have been given so much! I should work tirelessly to return thanks.
- I must be highly intelligent in order to be happy.
- I must be highly knowledgeable in order to find God.
- I must not relax; I must always be doing something productive.
- I cannot take time out to have fun; there are still so many important concerns to tend to.
- If something has to be done well, I must do it myself.
- I am somehow responsible for redressing all the world's wrongs.
- I must be strong for others!

Intensity

(Weak)			(Strong)	
1	2	3	4	5

4. Distorted Sense of Value: Based upon a misunderstanding of the meaning of certain values, it often derives from neglect of religious education or from theological ignorance. It leads to low self-worth, dependency, spiritual naïveté, frustration, confused thinking. Such a person is practically saying:

Intensity				
(Weak)			(Strong)	
1	2	3	4	5

- It would be selfish for me to assert my needs.
- If people really loved me they would know my needs without my speaking of them.
- To admit my strengths is egotistical.
- There is only one job in which I can be absolutely happy.
- There is only one person with whom I could be happily married.
- I can't pray; I'm certainly no saint.
- God will save the world. All I need to do is trust in him.
- Self-hatred is a healthy spiritual practice.
- Putting myself down in public is an example of true humility.
- I can never be happy in this world; I must wait for heaven.
- I must always expect the worst to happen and seek discomfort. This is my cross.
- God loves it when I suffer.
- Love means doing what other people want me to do.
- Just so long as I have loving intentions it doesn't matter what I do.

- When I no longer feel love for my spouse, it's OK to shop around.
- It is possible to be too virtuous; I must be careful about this.
- If people really loved me they would do what I want.
- I can do anything if I just put my mind to it.
- If I really love someone, I must never get angry at him/her.

5. **Materialism:** This leads to jealousy, envy, and avariciousness. It derives from spiritual neglect, media influences, and atheistic philosophies. Such a person is practically saying:

- I will finally be happy when I own certain possessions.
- Money is an accurate measure of a person's true worth.
- If it's free, it probably isn't worth striving for.
- No one can be poor and happy at the same time.
- I will finally be happy when I meet my financial goals.
- Wealthy people cannot be holy.

Intensity

(Weak)			(Strong)	
1	2	3	4	5

6. **Inferiority Complexes:** This leads to in-security, manipulative games, pro-crastination, perfectionism, loneliness, and burnout. It often derives from over-coercive parenting and past experiences of hurt. Such a person is practically saying:

- I must be absolutely sure of the outcome before I undertake a risky action.
- I must play games to impress people or they will not like me.
- I'm afraid that anything I start will turn out badly.
- I can't do anything right!
- I must be the center of attention in order to truly enjoy myself.
- I must be approved of by all; I must never be criticized.
- I must never make mistakes; when I do, it's the end of the world.
- People would not love me if they knew the real me.
- If I tried to explain myself, no one would really understand.
- It's always better to run from a problem than to face it.
- I must never upset other people.
- I'm too old to try anything new.
- I will not be lovable until I attain my ideal weight.

Intensity

(Weak)			(Strong)	
1	2	3	4	5

7. **Pessimistic Attitudes:** This means taking a negative and defensive view of reality. It derives from overindulgent parenting, past hurts, and nihilistic philosophies. It produces sour attitude, argumentation, factions, loneliness. Such a person is practically saying:

Intensity				
(Weak)			(Strong)	
1	2	3	4	5

- Why should I do anything? The world's going to get blown up soon anyhow.

- People don't want love, only sex.

- Life is an absurdity, for death is the end of everything.

- Considering all the suffering in the world, how can there be a good God?!

- All religious people are hypocrites! Why should I be like them?

- There is no such thing as good and evil; those are just relative terms.

- All truth is relative and provisional.

- I'm only going around once, so I'm grabbing for all the gusto I can get.

- Everybody's out to make big money; that's what it's all about.

- Beware of people who treat you kindly; they're after something.

- Big business runs the world; little people make no real difference.

- Communism, democracy: It's all the same thing.

- I can't please everyone so I have to look out for Number One first of all.

- If I trust people, they'll betray me first chance they get.

7

DIAGNOSE YOUR
ADDICTIONS

Any treatment of intrapersonal intelligence must of necessity examine addictive behavior. The reason is that many people suffer in this way and such addictions influence the operations of the mind.

Addiction refers primarily to alcoholism and drug dependencies; however, there are also addictions to other people, food, work, sex, gambling, overeating, and undereating. These are all very serious! Other common, and sometimes crippling, addictions include excess in the area of worrying, religious activity, shopping, watching television, playing video games, reading trashy books, and overuse of tobacco.

What, then, is meant by *addiction?* It is the compulsive use of any person, thing, or activity to meet your emotional and spiritual needs even though this causes abuse to you and others. The key words here are *compulsive* (it drives relentlessly) and *abuse* (it causes harm). A healthy person learns from mistakes and stops trying to meet emotional needs (acceptance, affirmation, security, validation, belonging) and spiritual needs (meaning, empowerment, ego-transcendence) in unhealthy ways. When you have an addiction, however, you persist in unhealthy behavior even though it causes harm.

In general, you will fall into addictive patterns when you use people, things, and activities to avoid dealing with your feelings. If you consistently smother your feelings, you will end up needing something or some activity to give you momentary pleasure and to numb your pain. This is the addictive "fix." Using alcohol when you are angry and tired is a prime example, but so are many other abusive actions. As a result of this cycle of smothering feelings and inappropriate release, you move deeper and deeper into the addictive process and add new addictions to your lifestyle. You become a zombie, numb — not quite dead, but not at all alive.

CHARACTERISTICS OF ADDICTS

You are in danger of becoming an addict if your lifestyle exhibits the following characteristics.

1. **Dishonesty.** This can include lying about your involvement in the area of concern or its extent and its consequences. It is also dishonest to pretend that nothing is wrong when something *is* wrong. Addicts ordinarily lie about their addictions.

2. **Self-centeredness.** Emotional pain creates a defense system which keeps you locked into yourself. Addiction and narcissism go hand-in-hand.

3. **Distorted perceptions.** You see hoses as snakes, other people as threats. Memory is distorted in that you block out discomfort and remember only the pleasurable parts of your addictive involvements.

4. **Faulty thinking.** You believe that you cannot exist without the object of your addiction, whether it be a thing (alcohol, food), a person (a lover, for example), or an activity (shopping, watching TV). You also believe you are no good because you cannot control your behavior.

5. **Emotional mismanagement.** Since you do not resolve your feelings, you frequently explode and/or blast people with "you

messages." You become very defensive about your addictive involvements, which blocks your ability to change.

6. **External orientation.** You focus on external cues rather than internal dynamics. Consequently, you blame others for your problems.

7. **Control fixation.** You seek to control your life and the lives of others through verbal and physical threats and abuse. The illusion of being able to control is common to all addictions, and it is one of the most difficult to overcome.

STAGES OF ADDICTION

The characteristics listed above describe chronic addiction. However, the addictive process can begin for you long before such deterioration takes place.

In the *initial stage,* you lock into one or more ways to meet your spiritual and emotional needs inappropriately. This "fix" gives you both relief and pleasure. But because you also start giving up healthy involvements, you are in the addictive process.

The *chronic stage* is characterized by the loss of many healthy involvements, an increase in emotional pain, and addictive involvements for the purpose of relieving pain. The fix no longer gives much pleasure so you go deeper into your addictions and add new addictions in an attempt to feel good. It is at this point that other people become aware that something is terribly wrong. Your health — physical, emotional, mental, and spiritual — is breaking down.

The *acute stage* features an almost complete loss of healthy consciousness as addictive processes completely take over the mind. In this stage there is no longer any relief from your pain, much less a euphoric fix.

The *terminal stage* is the death stage, wherein you use your addiction to obliterate consciousness. The alcoholic drinks to pass out; the co-dependent sits and simply stares, mumbling only monosyllables in response to questions.

ADDICTION AND CONSCIOUSNESS

It seems quite clear that addictions are entire states of consciousness operating in the psyche. They are consciousnesses within the larger total consciousness, each functioning as independent systems of perceiving, thinking, feeling, deciding, and behaving. At the center of the addictive circle of consciousness is the object of the addictive desires.

In the initial stage of addiction, the ego is not yet completely governed by addictions, and so you believe you can control your addictive involvements. It is in the initial stage that you learn the delusions of being in control and being able to manage your addictive involvements. By the time you reach the chronic stage, however, the ego is not able to separate itself from addictive processes. In the terminal stage, the entire psyche has been taken over by addictions. Patients in treatment for chemical dependency and co-dependency are often unable to demonstrate anything but addictive thinking and decision-making even after a month of intensive therapy. Addictions are extremely dangerous! They are, in truth, demons that cannot be overcome very easily.

Learning to recognize your addictive involvements and to discriminate between addictive and healthy thinking patterns is a critical task of intrapersonal intelligence. Applying the lessons you have learned so far can help you in this regard. It is fairly certain that anytime you are dishonest and/or repress your feelings, you fall into the addictive process.

To conquer your addictions it is necessary that you learn to meet your emotional and spiritual needs in a healthy manner. Intrapersonal and interpersonal intelligence can help you to meet your emotional needs. Spiritual growth processes such as the Twelve Steps of AA and the skills outlined in the book, *Pathways to Serenity,* can help you to meet your spiritual needs.

You are personally responsible for your own addictions, but it is likely that you will not recognize them without feedback from others. It is certain, too, that the support of other people will be needed if you are to grow out of addictive involvements. Getting involved in a support group is an excellent way to grow in intra- and interpersonal intelligence.

DAILY PRACTICES

1. Now that you have become more aware of your intrapersonal processes from the information presented in Chapters One through Six, what kinds of addictive patterns can you identify in yourself? To find out, answer the following questions:

   - When do I repress my feelings?
   - What do I do to get relief from emotional pain when I am tired, lonely, angry, or hurting?
   - What kinds of involvements do I tend to lie about?
   - What kinds of involvements am I uncomfortable with but have a hard time giving up?
   - What kinds of involvements are hurting me and others?
   - What kinds of involvements do I feel defensive about when confronted by others?
   - How difficult would it be for me to give up these involvements completely?

   In answering the above questions, do not focus only on your use of alcohol, drugs, sex, gambling, and food. Also consider other people, work, religious activities, worrying, shopping, watching television, excessive use of tobacco, sugar, chocolate, and the like. All of these can start you on the road to addiction.

2. If you realize — after the above drill — that you need help in certain areas, plan to attend an open meeting of one of the various peer support groups listed below. All are free and confidential. Call the number in the phone book for information about meetings in your area.

   - Alcoholics Anonymous. For people with drinking problems.
   - Al-Anon. For family and friends of alcoholics.
   - ACOA. For those who grew up in an alcoholic or otherwise dysfunctional family.
   - Alateen. For teenagers living with victims of alcoholism.
   - Narcotics Anonymous. For drug addicts.

- Narc-Anon. For family and friends of drug addicts.
- Overeaters Anonymous. For people with eating disorders.
- Gamblers Anonymous. For compulsive gamblers.
- Co-dependents Anonymous. For those who struggle with unhealthy relationships.
- Sex Addicts Anonymous. For those obsessed with sex.
- Victims of Sex Addicts Anonymous. For those who have been in relationships with sex addicts.
- Emotional Health Anonymous. For those who struggle with turbulent feelings.
- Parents Anonymous. For parents who struggle with discipline of their children.

8

REVIEW YOUR PAST

The writer of these pages once believed that it was unimportant to deal with the past. During that phase of his growth he believed that all he needed to do was to learn what has been discussed so far in Chapters One through Seven (which are all about how to live in the present), then formulate reasonable goals for the future. Little did he know that he would spend three long years dealing with the psychic implications of his own past as he wrestled with his own inner Shadow. (For the meaning of the Shadow state, see *Pathways to Serenity,* page 33.)

Perhaps you will find it very helpful to think of yourself not as a distinct unit but as many different selves. Actually, these are not different selves but different stages of self-development. This is not a radically new idea, of course. The proponents of Trans-actional Analysis have been speaking of parent, child, and adult selves for almost three decades now. The Jungians have also long recognized the many selves that live within individual persons — people met in dreams or even in waking consciousness. Perhaps the Pauline declaration (see 1 Corinthians 12:12-26) of the Mystical Body applies not only to the human family but to the individual as well.

HUMAN GROWTH PATTERNS

It is important that you always keep in mind those different people who live within you. Perhaps you imagine your past as stages of a rocket — each jettisoned so that the next can fly freely. Thus, you would have launched off in a first stage called infancy, which was discarded when a second stage called childhood fired up. Later came adolescence, young adulthood, the single life, the married years — and so you fly freely now, until this stage is jettisoned for the next. It doesn't work that way.

Actually, modern developmental psychology teaches that your growth is more like an onion than a rocket: you add layers around those you have already formed. There are times in life when you are supposed to learn certain lessons — lessons which enable you to grow into the next stage and learn what that time in life has to offer. As a child you are supposed to learn trust, autonomy, and industriousness; as an adolescent you learn to integrate experiences into an adult identity; as an adult you begin to understand the meaning of intimacy and how to stand on your own two feet; later you learn how to share with the larger world. If you do not learn these lessons, you are at a disadvantage in the next stage, and your growth becomes stunted until you find ways to learn them. You will have to re-parent certain aspects of your own inner child to learn lessons in intrapersonal intelligence that you missed along the way.

Many spiritual writers (especially those from the East) say that the past is dead. But this is true only if you have resolved all of your pain from the past. If your present feeling states bring up memories from the past, it is a sure sign that your past is not dead but is crying for reconciliation. Therapists are often amazed by how long an unresolved feeling can affect the lives of those seeking counseling. Grown adults will break down and cry when recounting experiences from childhood which were never resolved at the time. These feelings were continuing to influence these adults by locking them into addictive patterns. Unresolved pain from the early years is like a rotten spot inside an onion; it poisons the other layers which grow around it.

THE AWAKENED SELF

If you have followed the lessons and practices outlined in this book so far, you will already begin to see that you are not your thoughts, you are not your feelings, you are not your desires, and you are not your addictions. The fact that you can observe each of these psychic phenomena "from the outside" demonstrates that there is a YOU that is greater than the activities of your mind. YOU are that mysterious being who possesses a mind, but YOU are not your mind. Your mind belongs to YOU in the same manner as your body: it is part of YOU. *You are the loving awareness of your own consciousness.* This is your Christ-self. (See *Pathways to Serenity,* page 26.) Therefore, you are capable of learning to direct the activities of your consciousness in the ways of love.

With regard to your past, it is possible for YOU to relate with your past in a healing, nurturing manner. Consider, then, the following suggestions:

1. **Know yourself in your past.** Who were you in those days past? What have you learned? Practices such as those at the end of this chapter can help.

2. **Love the many selves within you.** Let them know that you accept them just as they are — even though they're a little muddled. Do not demand perfection from your past.

3. **Become aware of those times in your life when these different selves "stepped in" to run things for you.** Perhaps looking over some of your earlier practices can help you here.

4. **Make peace with your brokenness.** For example, when recalling a painful experience from childhood, YOU can now listen to and validate (two intrapersonal skills that will be treated later) your own inner child, which will speed the healing process.

Learning to love yourself means becoming a parent to your earlier selves. This is not an easy task. Like all parents, you must learn when it is appropriate to discipline or affirm your inner family. Always, however, you regard this family with unconditional acceptance and care.

Special Problems

Unfortunately, many of you may have experienced great pain during different stages of your lives. Perhaps there are inner selves that still cry out in anguish, for they have not been healed. Do what you can to become reconciled with these parts of your past, but also be willing to seek the help of a counselor or minister to support you. Perhaps an ACOA support group could also be helpful. Intrapersonal intelligence does not mean you have to do it all yourself. You do not get hurt by yourself nor do you heal alone.

Daily Practices

1. Get in touch with your inner selves. First, take a few minutes for quiet and relaxation. Be aware of your breathing. Offer yourself to God in prayer, and pray that you may be lovingly accepted.

2. Recalling that life unfolds in epochs (infancy, babyhood, childhood, adolescence, young adulthood through old age), and that within each epoch there are significant periods of growth and change, do the following:

   A. Select one period of your life to examine — one that you feel drawn to explore at this time. Understand that you do not have to complete this drill in one sitting.

      - Where did you live? Spend some time in memory moving around the house, seeing your bedroom, the kitchen, the yard, and so forth.
      - How did you spend your days? Let yourself relive a typical day.
      - How did you spend weekends? Make a list of hobbies/ pastimes.
      - How well did you relate with other family members?
      - Now, recall at least two pleasant experiences with other family members. Savor these experiences for a while.

Let yourself recall other experiences if they come naturally.

- Recall at least two unpleasant experiences you had with members of the family. What happened? How did you feel? If it becomes too painful to recall, share it with another person.
- How did you relate to God at this time in your life?
- What were some of the important lessons you learned about life during this period? How are these lessons influencing your life today?
- What were some of the unhealthy beliefs and habits you picked up during this period? (Consult the life-limiting belief survey at the end of Chapter Six for reflection here.) How are these habits still affecting you?
- Knowing what you know now, what would you like to say to the person who lived through those times? (Slowly, prayerfully, tell this person that you come from the future, and you have a message of hope and healing. Let yourself talk and listen to this person, continuing until the dialogue brings itself to a close.)
- Give this person a name (make up one of your own). Use this name when relating to that inner part of you. Tell this person you love him or her.

B. Do this same drill with some other epoch in your life.

9

PREPARE FOR YOUR FUTURE

"If you don't know where you're going, you'll probably get somewhere else" is an expression of recent vintage. This is true! Without goals, you are left at the mercy of the circumstances in which you find yourself. "Without a vision, the people perish," is another adage which applies here.

The most common way to face the future is to work toward goals. When you set goals, it is usually your hope that they point the way toward a better life for you. In terms of the intrapersonal dynamics discussed here, *goals can be seen as projections of your consciousness into the future.*

Not all goals are the same, however. In fact, some kinds of goals cause more problems than they resolve. Therefore, one of the tasks of intrapersonal growth is to become aware of the kinds of goals you have set for yourself. This chapter will discuss three types: compensatory, obligatory, and authentic. It is hoped that you will come to a time in life where all of your goals are authentic.

COMPENSATORY GOALS

Many people are living out of the past into the future. Their unresolved pain from the past influences their attitude about the future, and so they make decisions about the future on the basis of past experiences. This is only natural, of course. But if there is lack of emotional resolution in your own past experiences, then you will face the future with unhealthy biases. The goals you set are compensatory because they are unconscious attempts to make corrections for problems in the past.

Consider the following examples of goals gone awry. A certain man entered into a serious relationship with a young woman. But problems developed in their relationship which later in this book will be described as co-dependent and enmeshed. He tried to dominate her and she tried to dominate him. Because of this need to control, their relationship terminated in great emotional pain. The man learned nothing, however, for he placed the blame on the young woman for her immaturity. Consequently, he regarded future relationships with fear and uncertainty and found it very difficult to get close to women. His unresolved pain from that relationship prevented him from facing the future in freedom and hope. It wasn't until he did something like the exercises outlined in Chapters One through Eight that he realized he had the ability to take care of himself in a relationship no matter what the other person did. Only then was he free to let go of the need to control; only then could he love.

In general it can be said that too many people try to set goals without first learning who they really are. They pursue certain careers, completely unaware of their potential in the realms of their intrapersonal, interpersonal, and spiritual skills. Only later — when these skills become more apparent — do they realize how narrow were their first choices.

Other examples of compensatory goals are the following:

- A father who grew up in poverty determines to give his children lots of material things.
- A daughter of an alcoholic father who, because of her unresolved issues, marries an alcoholic "to try to love him into health."
- An oldest child in an alcoholic family who becomes an overachiever "to give this family some pride."

- A politician strives for more power "to get those who have hurt him."
- A worker who was once fired now fights to get to the top in order to control the company.

Most likely each of the people in these examples would find other values in their goals. But there can be no doubt that much of their energy derives from past hurts. When people live out of such compensatory goals, there is a strong possibility that they lose a sense of who they really are. In such cases they do not *have* goals; their goals have them.

OBLIGATORY GOALS

The chief characteristic of obligatory goals is that they are determined on the basis of others' expectations. Hence, they are not internally motivated as are compensatory and authentic goals. They are, most frequently, people-pleasing in nature.

Obligatory goals may derive from conscious and unconscious processes. A common example of an unconscious process can be seen in a young man who chooses a career that has been "encouraged" by his parents since early childhood. Such a youth may not even perceive that he really has other career choices! Indeed, every goal that is formulated to meet the expectations of parents, spouses, friends, and neighbors is obligatory in nature.

An example of a consciously formulated obligatory goal can be seen in the person who is concerned about "keeping up with the Joneses." The goals of such a person are determined by the lifestyle of the Joneses, and so they are external and obligatory in nature. If the Joneses get a new car or a swimming pool or add on a room to the house, this person sets a goal to do the same (or even to go "one-up" on them).

Obligatory goals lead to distorted growth. They should be identified in the best way possible, and then eliminated completely.

Authentic Goals

For healthy-minded people, goals emerge naturally from their self-understanding. They spring from personal inner truth and point the way to ongoing truth.

The author himself noticed this in his developing career as a writer. He discovered in his early twenties that he loved to write. Gradually, it dawned on him that this might be a good way to make a living. He then decided to learn more about writing as a profession, and set what he considered to be a reasonable goal to publish a book in the future. For years he submitted manuscripts to publishers, but all he received in return were rejection slips. He learned from these rejections, however, and gradually improved his writing ability until finally, in 1984, his first book was published. The joy of holding that book (*Becoming a New Person*, Liguori Publications) in his hands was one of the greatest of his life.

You will notice that when you are healthy in mind and body, goals emerge as a natural consequence of God's prompting. Your dreams will start coming true, and you will then set your goals accordingly. It is then possible to set objectives to help you to reach your goals. This writer's goal of one day publishing a book meant that he had to set objectives to learn how to write more clearly, and to submit his manuscript to a publisher in the proper way.

It is important, then, for you to strive to make all of your goals authentic. More than likely, you will discover that you have already set a number of goals on the basis of compensatory and obligatory factors. If that is so, then the two questions you need to ask are these: "Have I chosen this goal freely? Do I want to continue pursuing this goal?" It may be that your answer to the first question will be "no," but you will choose to do it anyway (in which case it has become an authentic goal). If your answer to both is "no," then you may choose to drop it.

At this point in your reading it is suggested that you set a goal to grow in intrapersonal and interpersonal intelligence. In doing so, it will become possible to discover your own authenticity, and your goals will become healthier.

When you put your personal growth first, the rest will follow.

Daily Practices

1. What are your dreams at this time in life?

   • If you had your choice of jobs, what would it be?
   • What would your ideal family situation be like?
   • Describe your ideal relationship with God.
   • What is your ideal overall lifestyle?
   Take a few moments and actually picture yourself living this way. Talk to the future self. Let it tell you what its life is like either in a written or imaginary dialogue.

2. How are these dreams related to your past? Can you see that any of them are compensatory or obligatory in nature?

3. What kinds of goals are you striving for at this time in your life?

4. As a result of your work in intrapersonal intelligence thus far, what new goals have you identified for yourself? What are the specific objectives necessary to attain those goals?

5. If you are not already doing so, set aside time each day for prayer and meditation. This will indicate that you are willing to allow God to influence your dreams for the future.

6. Pay more attention to your healthy interests and be willing to try out new experiences. During the coming month, resolve to try one healthy new experience that you have shunned in the past because you felt "that's not me."

10

SUMMARY

It is hoped that the first part of this book has made it clear that intrapersonal dynamics constitute a valid intelligence. In Chapters One through Nine the various intrapersonal dynamics have been identified and ways have been suggested to use these dynamics to grow in love of self. The primary focus has been to familiarize you with the nature of intrapersonal dynamics, rather than, say, with the outcomes of those dynamics.

It should be obvious that a growing familiarity with your own intrapersonal energies is much more beneficial in the long run than obtaining a temporary quick fix in one aspect of your growth. It is sad to see so many self-help books today which emphasize motivation along the lines of self-flattery and stress management. (Why don't they ever talk about stress elimination? That's also a possibility!) The fact that many of these books are best sellers only indicates how hungry people are for personal growth. What often happens, however, is that people set unhealthy goals and neglect unresolved pain in an effort to live as the author tells them they ought to live. They look upon these writers as gurus and fail to recognize the guru within each of themselves.

The primary objective in this section has been to teach you how your mind works, for this is the meaning of intrapersonal intelligence. Many people are trapped within their own minds because of addictions and unresolved pain. If you can learn to live with your own mind, then you will eventually discover for yourself what you need to do to meet your own needs.

Here, then, are a few general principles about intrapersonal intelligence.

1. You are the owner of your mind. You do not have to remain trapped in your small-selves because of addictions and unresolved pain.

2. You are capable of learning how your mind works and of untangling yourself from addictive patterns. This is not accomplished through willful control, however; it is a result of loving and forgiving yourself into freedom.

3. You are responsible for your own behavior and for the functioning of your mind. Even if other people have mistreated you and forced you into addictive patterns, it is now your responsibility to take care of yourself.

Daily Practices

To continue growing in these lessons, it is recommended that you occasionally reread the chapters in this section and repeat these practices again from time to time. Another way to continue growing is to join a support group that allows you to work on all of the relationship skills. But in the ordinary events of everyday life, here are two practices that are essential for growth in intrapersonal intelligence.

1. **Strive for present-moment awareness.** Stop often in the day to check in with yourself in the manner described below.

    A. As I notice what's going on around me, what are my senses picking up?

B. What am I feeling about what's happening? Try to give the feeling state a label.

C. When feelings become intense, ask:
- How will I express these feelings?
- What are my thoughts and expectations?
- Are they legitimate? Reasonable?

2. **Make a daily consciousness examen.** This one requires a bit of work each day, but it simply needs doing. Try it for thirty days; it will change your life.

   A. Set aside at least fifteen minutes in the evening to review your day. Doing this work in a journal is healthy. It may also be done while taking a slow, relaxing walk.

   B. Begin with prayer, inviting God to help you to see yourself as God saw you today. Be willing to be very honest with yourself.

   C. Slowly review your day. If you are emotionally in touch with one part of your day, begin there. Otherwise, start at the beginning and work through. Consider the following:

   - What happened? This does not have to be a minute-by-minute review; a general one will do.
   - What was going on within me? What were my thoughts, feelings, desires, decisions?
   - How do I feel now about my states of consciousness through these events? (Acknowledge the feelings you experienced, affirm yourself for the good, and confront your irresponsible behaviors.)
   - Is there anyone I've hurt or anything I've done that needs to be corrected? (Plan to make amends.)

- Is there anything I'd do differently if I had to do it over? (If so, relive this incident in imagination, only now with healthy thoughts, decisions, and behavior. See and feel this new way of acting on your part.)

D. Final question: What did I learn about myself today?

E. Close with a prayer of gratitude for the gifts generally taken for granted (health, family, and so forth), and pray for the grace of a good sleep.

PART TWO

INTERPERSONAL INTELLIGENCE: RELATING WITH OTHERS

Interpersonal intelligence refers to your ability to read the feelings, intentions, and desires of others — even when hidden — and to act upon this knowledge. "What's happening in the other person?" is its first concern; and from this follows the second, "How do I want to act on this knowledge?"

Keeping this definition in mind, notice that interpersonal intelligence is by no means synonymous with loving other people. Simply being able to read the feelings, intentions, and desires of others does not mean that you will lovingly act on this knowledge. Politicians are constantly examining polls about people's feelings and desires in order to use them for their own purposes (which are not always loving). That is why in this section every effort is made to study the interpersonal skills with the idea of putting them to use in the service of love.

It has been said many times that no one is an island. Children do not come into this world by themselves, nor do they sustain themselves in isolation. It is in the context of relationships that basic needs — physical, mental, spiritual, and emotional — are met.

Although you use relationships to meet most of your needs, the focus in this section is on the manner in which relationships help you to meet your emotional needs. These needs have been mentioned several times throughout this work. They include acceptance, affirmation, approval, security, belonging, and intimacy. You can accord to yourself a certain amount of acceptance, affirmation, approval, and security; but it is much better if you are doing this with others, too. It is impossible, however, to experience belonging and intimacy in isolation. By growing in interpersonal intelligence, you learn how to connect yourself with others so as to experience a heightened sense of belonging and intimacy. Learning how to do this may well be your most urgent need in today's world.

Types of Personal Relationships

There are four types of personal relationships: parallel independent, co-dependent-counterdependent, enmeshed, and interdependent. It is possible to experience all of these four types at different times in life; but most relationships generally assume only one of these four patterns.

A *parallel independent relationship* exists when two basically whole people (see Figure One) abide with each other but do not share very much on an emotional level. Examples of this would be

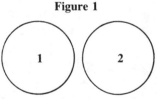

Figure 1

two healthy people living together merely for financial reasons. Two marriage partners fully involved in careers might also drift into this pattern. While this coexistence may be peaceful, it does not meet the needs for belonging and intimacy.

Much more common is the *co-dependent-counterdependent relationship* (see Figure Two). Here, one person (call her Jane) is co-dependent on another person (call him Tom), who is rigidly anti-dependent. Tom has a sense of boundaries and independence in this relationship, but Jane does not. She defines her health in relationship to Tom; if he's OK, she's OK; if he's angry, she's angry. If Jane and Tom were to divorce, Jane would be left with a gaping emotional wound which, typically, she would try to fill with another relationship or through compulsive activities like excessive eating, drinking, working, or inordinate use of

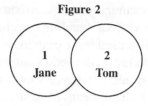

Figure 2

sex. Typically in these relationships, Tom would be involved in an addiction of some kind and would be using Jane to support this addiction; her support of his addiction is called "enabling" in the field of chemical dependency. To stay in this relationship, Jane focuses on Tom's behavior, gives up her own enjoyments, and loses herself in the process.

Enmeshed relationships (see Figure Three) happen when two people focus so intensely on each other that they lose a sense of boundaries. This happens when two co-dependents join together. It also occurs in dysfunctional families where each person is emotionally affected by the other. In these relationships, people experience emotional connectedness; they often talk about how close they really are. However, this is only a negative intimacy be-

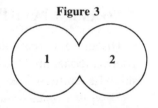

Figure 3

cause there are no boundaries between the two people. There is also no emotional freedom; what one feels, the other feels. Consequently, people in these relationships are unable to truly love one another because they all get caught up in each other's emotional problems.

Interdependent relationships (see Figure Four) happen when two healthy people come together freely to share emotional energy (pleasant or unpleasant) with each other. There is both separateness and togetherness in this relationship. If one is angry, the other is free to listen and acknowledge these feelings without getting angry, too. Their love comes out of strength, not an addictive need to find completion in each other. This is the most satisfying form of relationship, for in it

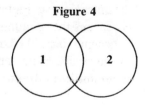

Figure 4

you can meet your emotional needs without losing yourself. It is this pattern which is being encouraged in this book.

It is a sad fact that there are too few interdependent relationships in today's culture. Traditionally, society has defined the perfect marriage as one in which two people cannot live without each other. This means enmeshment. Enmeshments and co-dependency characterize most of today's love songs — especially country and western and rock music. Small wonder so many people have disappointing relationships!

These positive and negative patterns are found everywhere. Teachers often give advice that — if followed — would produce enmeshments. Putting others first might be good advice to give a hedonist, but it is death to a co-dependent. Stressing commitment in bad times and good will help impatient young couples, but it is of no help to a battered wife.

TWO IMPORTANT PRINCIPLES

Through the years you have learned how to communicate in your relationships. But as you examine this area of your life you should keep these two principles in mind:

1. **Your communication determines the shape of your relationships.** You learned your communication skills in the context of a prevailing pattern of relationships, and so you continue to communicate for those types of relationships. But if you are like most people in today's culture, you have picked up a few unhealthy interpersonal skills along the way.

2. **You control your terms for relating with others.** You cannot control the behavior of others, but you can control how you relate to them. For example, you decide that you will no longer enter into co-dependent and enmeshed relationships. This means that you have to quit trying to control people, and you can no longer take responsibility for their problems. Likewise, you cannot be in an interdependent relationship with someone (even a healthy-minded person) who chooses not to share very much with you. No matter how much you share, you cannot

control the response of the other. The best you can hope for in this case is parallel independence — not the worst situation at all.

The skills presented in this second part of the book are intended to help you build interdependent relationships. It will be impossible, however, for you to grow in these skills if you are not also growing in intrapersonal intelligence and in your spiritual health. Because you already know a manner of communicating, you will continue to act in that manner unless you change from within. "Love your neighbor as *yourself*," is an apt description of interdependent relationships.

11

RESISTING THE TEMPTATION TO SHAME OTHERS

Interpersonal intelligence is concerned with two issues: What you see going on in the other person and how you relate to that knowledge. This chapter and the following one address the second issue; the first issue will be treated in Chapter 13.

LEVELS OF RELATIONSHIPS

There are four different levels of relationships. First in importance is the level of those people with whom you share your life most intensely, that is, your family and closest friends. Secondly, there are those with whom you share much of yourself during the course of work and play — friends, co-workers, and extended family members. A third level would include people you know and encounter occasionally, but for a superficial kind of interaction. Finally, there are those whom you do not know and do not relate with in any significant kind of personal interaction. In the course of time, people move in and out of all four levels: superficial acquaintances become good friends; co-workers move away and communication ceases.

People in first- and second-level relationships have a profound influence upon one another. It is in such relationships that your needs for intimacy are met. Third and fourth level relationships are also important, but they do not affect you as deeply. If you are criticized by a complete stranger, you may tell him or her where to get off and think of it no longer. But criticism from a person you rub shoulders with daily is another matter altogether. As you live and interact with people in first- and second-level relationships, you are constantly communicating to one another an evaluation of both personhood and behavior. Like mirrors, you reflect back to one another a wide range of evaluations. These fall into three general categories:

	Personality	Behavior
1. Affirmation	✔	✔
2. Discipline/Confrontation	✔	✘
3. Shaming	✘	✘

As the accompanying chart indicates, affirmation — the first possibility — comments positively on personality and behavior. Its message is, ''I like who you are and I like what you're doing.'' If internalized by the other, affirmation can lead to an increase in self-worth and self-confidence.

A second possibility is discipline or confrontation. ''I like you, but right now there is need to discuss certain behaviors of yours which bother me,'' reads this evaluation. (Because learning to affirm and confront are so vitally important in relationships, they will be treated more fully in later chapters.)

The third possibility is shaming, which berates both personality and behavior. ''I don't like you and I don't like what you're doing,'' reads the message of shame. Its internalization makes the other person think, ''I'm no good and I can't do anything right.'' Shaming leads to low self-worth and low self-confidence — two factors which have been correlated with alcohol/drug abuse, suicidal tendencies, sexual irresponsibility, criminal behavior, and relationship failures. These are devastating situations which are often brought on by the shaming of others.

EXAMPLES OF SHAMING

When are you guilty of shaming others? *This happens any time you communicate negatively about their personhood.* Listed below are a few examples of shaming tactics as described in the book, *Building Character in Young People,* (Pelican Publishing Co., 1986).

1. **Comparing.** "Why can't you be more like so-and-so?" Comparisons imply that people are not acceptable in themselves.

2. **Labeling.** "She's a slow learner." "He's the black sheep of the family." Names like "stupid," "dummy," or worse are also examples. Labeling restricts your openness to the fullness of possibilities present in another person.

3. **Dumping.** By this is meant unloading your anger and frustration on others when you are really angry about something else. When you augment your anger, others perceive that they have brought on the full intensity of your distaste. Dumping that results in physical abuse is especially shaming.

4. **Condescension.** This happens when you talk down to others or patronize them. Even if this is well-intentioned (which it generally isn't), condescension fails to recognize the dignity of the other. While it is true that there are inequalities in behavioral skills, intelligence, and other potentialities among people, this should not lead you to conclude that there is also an inequality of dignity.

5. **Judgmentalism.** Judgments are statements about people's motives (generally their uglier ones). Calling people bad or good is an example. Judgment of this sort belongs only to God. Judgment is usually accompanied by such absolute statements as "always" and "never."

6. **Profanity.** "When you get angry, count to four; when you get very angry, swear." This quip from Mark Twain is humorous, but swearing at other people in anger is not.

7. **Negative Attitudes.** This does not refer to bad moods, but to that cynicism and negativity which says to the other, "I'm not glad to be here with you."

8. **Neglect.** Taking others for granted, avoiding them, and spending little time with them can only lead them to conclude that you do not care for them. People who neglect first- and second-level relationships are really saying "You're so unimportant, I won't even pay attention to you." The opposite of love is not hate, but apathy and indifference, which lead to neglect.

Other communication habits which may involve shaming to some degree include *nagging, sarcasm, interrupting, continually talking about yourself, criticizing someone in front of others, giving advice when it is not asked for, gossiping, and scorning others.* At issue here are not your motives (for they may be very good), but the probable consequences of these kinds of communications. Parents sometimes say that they criticize their children to motivate them to try harder at something. But shaming is very poor communication, as can be seen from the following:

- As an indirect mode of communication, it does not allow you to clearly express what you are feeling.
- The person who receives a shaming communication from you will react more to the negative communication than to the issue you are addressing. Shaming adds new issues to an already difficult situation.
- Shaming communication on your part reinforces you negatively in *your own* perceptions, beliefs, feelings, and decisions. This will kill the warmth of love within you.
- Shaming contributes to attitudinal and behavioral problems in others.

Therefore, your first rule in loving others is this: If you cannot make things better, then at least do not make them worse. Thou shalt not shame thy brothers and sisters! Never! Not for any reason is shaming ever justified! You probably learned to do this because it was done to you. But there are more effective ways to express your feelings, so you will have to learn to program those ways into your behavioral repertoire.

DAILY PRACTICES

1. Make a list of people with whom you share first-level involvements.

   A. Why are these people important to you?

   B. What kinds of activities do you share with them on a regular basis?

   C. How would you feel if you were to lose these people?

   D. How often do you communicate in a shaming manner to each of these people? (For each of the shaming practices listed below, indicate frequency: N - Never; S - Seldom; F - Frequently; V - Very Frequently.)

   _____ Comparing   _____ Neglect
   _____ Labeling   _____ Sarcasm
   _____ Dumping   _____ Criticism
   _____ Condescension   _____ Advising
   _____ Judgmentalism   _____ Interrupting
   _____ Profanity   _____ Scorning
   _____ Negative Attitudes

   E. How do your shaming communications affect these people? (Picture yourself in the place of one of them and imagine receiving a shaming comment from you.)

   F. If you are brave and other people are willing, ask them to review your shaming behavior survey and tell you how they feel when you do these things. Do not contest what they say. Simply listen and learn.

2. Follow the above procedure with your second- and third-level relationships.

3. When you become aware that you are about to shame someone, take a deep breath and resolve that you will not do so. Express your feelings by using the "I message." Future chapters will teach you alternative ways to confront and discipline; but, for now, it is simply enough that you resist the temptation to shame. Also, refrain from shaming yourself.

12

REFUSING TO DO FOR OTHERS WHAT THEY SHOULD DO FOR THEMSELVES

Here is a story about a father and his eight-year-old daughter named Rita. One day she asked him to tie her shoes for her. As he was operating on what might be called "automatic pilot" (doing what needs to be done without thinking much about it), he bent down and began to tie one of the shoes. After he had tied that first one, it suddenly occurred to him that she had been tying her own shoes for over two years. "So what am I doing on my knees before this little girl?" he asked himself.

"Rita, you know how to tie your own shoes," he commented. "Why do you want me to do them for you?"

"I don't know," she shrugged. "I just didn't feel like tying them myself today."

He thought this over for a few seconds. Maybe she just wants pampering and a little attention and this is how she's asking for it. Children don't always know what they really need — even as many adults don't know. Nevertheless, there's a lesson to be taught here.

After completing the first shoe, he moved over to sit next to Rita, and he hugged her close. "There, now, I've tied one shoe, but you can do the other one. In fact, this will be the last shoe I ever tie for you unless you really need me to do it," he explained. "When you were a little girl I had to do this all the time, but now. . . . "

"Then how come you still tie Theresa's shoes?" she broke in.

"Theresa's only five. She can't tie her own shoes. When she can tie them herself, I won't do it for her anymore. When you were five, Mom or I tied them for you every day."

She remained silent for a moment, puzzling over this strange consequence of getting older. "It's not fair," she finally lamented. "She gets more attention than me."

It's true, of course: Little people and dependent people do get more attention. "The squeaky wheel gets the grease."

"You're right, Rita," he agreed. "But because you're older, we can also do things together that I can't do with Theresa."

"Like what?" she objected.

He then proceeded to list various games and activities that she does better than Theresa because she is older. After a while she felt better — if for no other reason than she'd gotten some of the attention she'd been seeking. (Incidentally, she tied her second shoe herself.)

This story illustrates perfectly the second guideline for growing in relationships with others: *Refuse to do for others what they should do for themselves*. (However, an occasional surprise is not out of place.) At first glance this may appear to be heartless, but it is not so, as the statements listed below explain:

• You *must* do for others what they cannot do for themselves.
• You *may*, as a surprise, do for others the work that they can do for themselves. This is also an excellent way to show support for them.

This guideline, then, does not negate helping, surprising, supporting, and serving. Instead, it attempts to recognize the importance of respecting the freedom and dignity of others.

YOUR RESPONSIBILITY

If you feel that you must always be your brother's keeper, you should reexamine that phrase. Note that you are not responsible *for* one another, but *to* one another. There's a big difference. If you are responsible for others' behavior, then you are also somehow responsible for rectifying their mistakes. This is ridiculous, of course. If, instead, you are responsible to others, then you identify yourself as one who is free to choose your involvements with others.

God treats you in much the same way. He allows you to experience the consequences of your actions, for you would fail to learn if you did not do so. God does not want you to hurt yourself and others, but he also respects your freedom and dignity so much that he does not impose, but awaits your responses to his loving invitations.

If you frequently do for others what they can and ought to do for themselves, you reinforce dependency. You can note examples of this kind of dependency — caretaking in some parents with their children, some wives with their alcoholic husbands, and governments with some of their welfare recipients. Little help is really given in these cases, although the helper believes it is the best way to "control" a difficult situation. But, in truth, the helper feels frustrated over energy vainly expended, and the helpee feels resentful over being treated as a dependent and, hence, irresponsible person. It seems that only a few get better while many get worse because of this misguided understanding of being your brother's keeper.

It should be noted that this guideline does not absolve you from striving for social justice. Being responsible to others calls for working to change situations that increase selfishness and dependency in today's world. You cannot just say to the poor and underprivileged: "God helps those who help themselves." On the other hand, of course, you cannot favor a welfare system which reinforces dependency by punishing recipients who undertake initiatives for responsibility. Being responsible to others means that you must own up to your part in helping to create an environment that invites and supports human growth.

SORTING THE ISSUES

In applying this guideline to your interpersonal relationships, it is a good practice to ask: "Whose issue is this?" For example, if your children or family members are bickering, you might ask this question. If it is their problem, then mind your own business. This is especially important for parents and children. Too often parents want to enter their children's disputes and settle things for them. Instead, they should avoid entering the dispute until it becomes absolutely clear that someone else is needed to facilitate dialogue between them. Parents, of course, have a right to let their children know when their dispute is disturbing the household. But children will learn nothing about conflict resolution if their parents step in and take over the first moment bickering breaks out.

Another way to show respect for the freedom and dignity of others is to allow them to experience the consequences of their actions. It is a false love that shields and protects people from consequences. An example: The police in a certain city rounded up a group of minors who were drinking and disturbing the peace while on a school trip. Rather than thank the police, which they should have done, the parents of these students lambasted them in newspaper articles and press conferences. These parents seemed much more concerned about their own social images than about their youngsters' drinking. And these young people failed to learn their lesson from the experience.

So, no more controlling, manipulating, and protecting people from reality. Reality is a very good teacher, even though its lessons are sometimes painful. And what's true of your relationships with others is also true of theirs with you. You have a right to experience the reality of your own life without being controlled, manipulated, and protected by others.

DAILY PRACTICES

1. After looking over your prior entries, answer this question and do the following:

   A. Do any of your shaming practices spring from frustrations caused by your attempts to control, manipulate, and protect others? If so, confront these erroneous beliefs and imagine what things would be like if you were to let go of those expectations. Imagine yourself in these new and freer relationships. Experience the new feelings of relief.

2. Are any of your shaming practices rooted in frustration over your perception of being controlled by other people? If so, answer the following questions:

   A. How do you see each person trying to control you? Be specific.

   B. How do you generally respond to their controlling?

   C. What kind of dependency does it create in you?

   (Later in this second part you will learn a way of sharing this information with others. For now, simply be in touch with it.)

3. Get used to asking the question: "Whose issue is this?" If it belongs to others, then let it be; if it concerns you, then accept your part in it and become involved.

13

LISTENING WITH ALL YOUR HEART

Your first concern in the area of interpersonal intelligence — as stated in Chapter Eleven — is to find out what is happening in the other person. The reason it was not treated first is because it is impossible to really enter into the experiences of others so long as you are intent on shaming, manipulating, controlling, and directing them (as described in the two previous chapters). When you do these things, you are not interested in people for their own sakes but for yours. You see the others not as separate individuals but as mere extensions of your own egos. Included here are those parents who pride themselves on their children's achievement (when, very often, the children are not interested in the activity at all, but do it only to please their parents). It is probably impossible to completely eliminate selfishness in relationships, but you can make great progress by practicing the suggestions in Chapters Eleven and Twelve.

This points out the importance of listening to others — another excellent way to rid yourself of selfishness. When you listen — really listen — to others, you acknowledge the fact of their individuality and the uniqueness of their experiences. One of the best ways to love people is to listen to them. Listening also opens for you the possibility of encountering the God who lives and moves and has his being in the other.

HOW TO LISTEN

But what is meant by listening? First of all, it is not simply biding your time in silence before another. There is a kind of silence that is part of listening, but there is another that is impatient and preoccupied. Many times while in conversation with others you may find yourself not really listening but waiting to talk. This is only natural, for perception is both sensate and intuitive. But silence that is characterized by attentiveness to your own intuitive responses is listening to self, not others.

When you are with others, then, it is fitting that you pay attention to your intuitive responses to them. However, listening requires that you also focus your attention on the sensate data coming from the other, especially through sight and sound. It is estimated that 75% of communication is nonverbal. Therefore you use your eyes to note body language, tiredness/alertness, clothing, facial expressions, eye color, gesturing, and other such things. You use your ears to hear the sound of the voice, emotional undertones, interest/avoidance, and so forth. Only after you are in sensate contact with the other should you begin to pay attention to your intuitive responses. Even then, however, you must make an effort to keep intuition trained on the needs of the other rather than self. A loving intuition asks: "What's really going on in this person?" "What does the other really want from me?" "How can I best help this person?"

Another way to understand the dynamics of listening is to consider the equation reflected upon in Part One: that your behavior derives from the decisions you made in light of the perceptions monitored by your beliefs, feelings, and desires.

As you listen to others you use your senses and intuition to get in touch with *their* perceptions, beliefs, feelings, and decisions. In doing so, you discover who they are and why they do the things they do. Getting in touch with a person in this manner is a very powerful experience. It is like crawling into their skin to see what they see, hear what they hear, feel what they feel, and so forth.

MAKING THE EFFORT

Listening to other people in the manner discussed here is an active occupation and not a passive one. It takes work to keep your attention trained on another. You can even become exhausted from listening to a very gifted lecturer. If you are already tired, your mind will keep wandering away from the speaker, even though he or she is addressing a topic very important to you. After the talk, friends may remark on how tired you look, and you tell them yes, you've been through a long day and sitting and listening has worn you out even more. "But you've been sitting down and resting all this time!" they object, invalidating your experience. Resting, indeed! Real listening calls for dying to self and that's never restful for anyone.

Although listening can be tiring, it can also lead to new energizing experiences. Listening to a good lecture is tiring, but afterward when the words have penetrated (which they cannot do unless you listen), the fruits of listening can be noted in a fuller experience of others, yourself, God, and life in general. In time, listening skills can also become habitual. Your attention is like a wild horse that needs to be trained to obey its master — you! It *can* be trained. It *must* be trained. The suggestions in the following Daily Practices can help you to do it.

DAILY PRACTICES

1. Look back over three conversations you had with people during the past day. Were you listening — really listening to them? If so, what did you learn about them? About yourself? If not, what was going on inside you that prevented you from listening?

2. Take fifteen minutes every day or two to sit outside and simply listen to life. What do you see? Smell? Hear? Feel on your skin? Focus your attention on these sensate data while being aware of your intuitive responses. Resist, however, the temptation to get lost in plans, dreams, worries, and thoughts. Just be there with your senses.

3. When conversing with others — especially concerning important issues, make an effort to pay attention to them. Note their physical expressions and tones of voice. Focus your intuition on what they're really saying, what they really need from you, and how you can best respond.

14

VALIDATING AND CLARIFYING

Have you ever listened to those talk show hosts taking calls from all over the country? If so, you must have noticed how often they use words like these: "So what you're saying is . . . " or "So you felt . . . " or "Let me see if I understand what you just said: I heard you saying. . . . " These are great ways to validate and clarify the experiences of others while listening to them. This practice is perhaps the most important interpersonal communication skill. It is also the most neglected in everyday life.

VALIDATING SKILLS

When you validate you confirm others by simply acknowledging their experiences and accepting them without judgment. Your words say to a person: "Yes, yes, so this is what happened, and this is how you felt. I understand." The person who is validated in this manner feels accepted and understood, which may open the possibility of deeper communication. It is also a fact that many times all people really want is to be heard and validated. This, then, is an excellent way to show them your love.

The skill of validating others is exercised by paying attention to them and listening for their feelings. (It is important to validate opinions, too.) As they speak, you reassure them that you are listening by occasionally nodding and saying words such as

"Yes," or "I see," or "I understand" (even "Uh-huh" is acceptable at times). These simple words are actually saying, "I'm with you; go on; keep talking." As you pick up their feelings, you let them know occasionally by saying, "So you felt (name the emotion) when . . . " Validating does no more than this! Empathizing, risking, affirming, negotiating, and confronting come later.

Validation, after all, is simply an "I message" in reverse. The best way to teach children to express feelings appropriately is to validate them. This gives them a feeling word to describe their own experiences. If you tell your crying three-year-old, "Looks like you're really sad about losing your doll," she learns that *sad* is the name of that feeling of loss. (A hug would go well here, too.)

To sum up, validation is a tool you can use to help others grow in intrapersonal intelligence. By validating the feelings of others, you help them to identify their feelings, label them, and relate them to other psychic processes. In addition, you let them know that you are with them in their feelings — that you understand. It is a marvelous skill to make others realize that they are not alone.

INVALIDATING PRACTICES

Far too often, people not only fail to validate, but they also *invalidate* the experiences of others. Recall the example in Chapter Thirteen about your friends who told you that you shouldn't have felt tired because you had been sitting down (and presumably resting) while listening to a lecture. Your thoughts at that time may have been: "I don't care what *you* think! I *am* tired! I don't need you to tell me how to feel!" Invalidation destroys communication. Here are some other ways people use when they invalidate others:

1. **Discounting.** "You shouldn't feel that way." Or "You're wrong about that feeling!" Nonsense! People feel what they feel.

2. **Pressuring.** "Don't feel that way." This usually indicates the listener's discomfort with a particular feeling (anger, crying) rather than concern about the other's emotional state.

3. **Advising.** There is a time and a place for offering advice, but not until the other person has really been heard and there is certainty that he or she wants advice.

4. **Diagnosing.** Trying to get others to understand why they feel as they do. This, too, may be appropriate, but only after validation.

5. **Ridiculing.** Laughing at another's feelings is the ultimate invalidation.

6. **Changing the subject.** This indicates that the listener may not have been really listening, but only waiting to say something.

7. **Remaining silent.** Simply not talking about feelings or emotional issues is invalidating. Parents who keep silent before their children about obvious emotional issues, or who even deny their feelings cause terrible emotional confusion.

8. **Negating.** "You aren't really mad, are you?" This tells others they aren't really experiencing their feelings.

Many invalidating practices derive from the assumption that it is bad to have certain feelings. Such a view is not only unwarranted but positively harmful. Feelings are neither bad nor good in themselves. To validate the feelings of others, therefore, has nothing to do with judging people. It merely acknowledges the emotional reality of situations brought to your attention through listening.

CLARIFYING SKILLS

The skill of clarifying is practiced by occasionally checking with the other to make sure you understand what is being related. Because it's impossible to validate what you don't understand, it is sometimes helpful to ask for a fuller explanation of important experiences when you're not sure what the other is saying. Two good opening phrases for clarification are listed below:

1. "So what you're saying is (here recite what you think they are saying). Is that right?" If it's not right, the other will usually feel free to respond.

2. "I'm not sure I understood what you meant when you said (here give your understanding of what was said). Could you help me out with that?"

As the other clarifies the experience, it is a good time to validate him or her.

You will find that if you take more time to clarify issues, you will probably reduce your conflicts with others by 50% or more. Very often you react to what you think the other said or meant, when this was not the intention at all. Remember, a person's reality begins with his or her perception. Because one person's intentions do not always match the other's perceptions, it is essential to clarify experiences as much as possible.

It is especially important that you use clarifying skills before confronting or disciplining another. This is called checking. Suppose, for example, that you as a mother ask your daughter, Sandra, to clean her room before company comes. A few minutes later you pass by and see that Sandra is gone and the room is still a mess. Feeling angry about this, you storm outside and ask Sandra to come in and clean her room like you had asked her to.

"I cleaned it already!" she replies, somewhat hurt that you hadn't noticed.

Fortunately, you remember to check her perceptions, so you ask: "Sandra, what did you think I meant when I asked you to clean your room?"

"I thought you wanted me to pick up my clothes," she returns, still defensive.

She had done this.

"Well, Sandra, I wanted more than that. I also wanted you to pick up your toys and make your bed, but I guess you didn't know that, did you?"

She shrugs in agreement, happy to be off the hook, but not at all enthused about doing these additional chores.

"Next time I'll know to tell you exactly what I mean," you offer, "and if you don't understand, will you please let me know?"

Sandra was not born with a clear understanding of what is meant by the words, "clean your room." This is also true of other people with whom you converse daily. That is why it is important to clarify perceptions, beliefs, feelings, and decisions — especially regarding abstract matters.

DAILY PRACTICES

1. Look back over three conversations you had with people during the past day. Were you listening to them? How did you validate their experiences? Did you invalidate them? Would it have been helpful to clarify matters a little better?

2. Review the invalidating practices described in this chapter. When you become conscious of doing one of them, resist it. Validate instead.

3. Add these validating skills to your conversational repertoire.

   A. "I'm with you." "Yes, yes." "I see."

   B. "I understand." "You were (mention a feeling adjective), right?" "So you felt (mention a feeling noun) because . . . , right?"

4. When uncertain about the feelings or intentions of another, use these clarifying phrases: "So what you're saying is (give your perception). Is that right?" "I'm not sure I understand what you meant by (repeat the phrase/experience). Can you help me out with this?" "What do you mean by (mention word, phrase, experience)?"

5. Before confronting or disciplining others, remember to check their perceptions and intentions about the matter at hand.

15

EMPATHIZING

"I know exactly how you feel." How many times have you heard those words? When you yourself say them to others, you are empathizing with them.

Some human relations teachers state that the above phrase is inaccurate, for you cannot possibly know what another is really feeling. They're probably right, but there's no doubt that all persons possess the capability to understand the feelings of others. Every human being knows what it's like to be mad, sad, glad, and scared at times. When others express these feelings, everyone knows what they're saying. Maybe the better way to respond would be, "So you were sad (or some other emotional word) when that happened. I know what it's like to feel that way." It may then be appropriate for you to share your experience.

EMPATHIZING SKILLS

People often ask if there is a difference between empathizing and sympathizing. In truth, the dictionary definitions are almost the same, but most people think of sympathizing as feeling sorry for another. As such, sympathizing would not be a relationship skill, but a specific feeling — a kind of sadness. *Empathizing, on the other hand, refers to your capacity to feel with others and to let them know that you have experienced what they are feeling.*

Empathy makes it possible for you to become real to another person. When children complain that they don't like school and don't feel like going, they are amazed to learn that their parents felt the same way at their age. If you as a parent share with them other experiences from your childhood — especially times when you felt angry, embarrassed, and confused — you can help them to realize that you weren't born an adult, that you, too, were once a child, and that lots of children feel exactly as they do.

For a number of reasons you may find it especially difficult to believe that other people have the same unpleasant feelings that you have. One of the consequences of unpleasant feelings is that they turn you in on yourself, leading to self-preoccupation. It is easy during these times to conclude that no one has ever felt like you do, and that no one would understand what you're going through if you told them. When you are in such a state, it helps to be listened to and validated, but it is not until you also experience empathy from others that you can let go of your preoccupations and give of yourself again.

This, no doubt, is the secret behind the successes of the many peer-support, self-help groups today. In these groups, people with similar problems come together and, if nothing else, learn that they are not alone, that they are not weird, that others have had the same frenetic thoughts and experienced the same unpleasant feelings. This in itself is a truly liberating experience. It is not uncommon to hear people remarking after their first group meeting, ''Gee! And I thought I was the only one who felt that way.''

In addition, peer-support groups offer guidance on how to break free from compulsions and self-preoccupation and begin to live again. (In *Becoming a New Person: Twelve Steps to Christian Growth,* Liguori Publications, 1984, and in *How to Form a Christian Growth Support Group,* Liguori Publications, 1985, the author proposes the use of the Twelve Steps of peer-support groups as an aid in overcoming common selfishness and in growing into a more loving person.)

Empathizing as a skill can be exercised only after you have been listening, clarifying, and validating. Even then, you must be careful to avoid using empathy to turn the conversation your way. You have probably at some time had this experience. People begin to empathize, but then they begin telling their own story, leaving you feeling cut off. This temptation should be resisted unless you see that the other is genuinely interested. Even then, however, it is good manners to first inquire if they have finished what they have to say.

EMPATHY AND INTIMACY

Empathy is a peculiar skill in that it is not only a way of responding to others but also a way of reading their feelings and intentions. Effective empathizing helps others to open up and share more of themselves, which gives you an even better understanding of who they are. It is one of the foremost connecting skills. At its best, empathizing leads to a round of intimate storytelling: "That reminds me of the time . . . ," or "Did I ever tell you the one about . . . ?" In telling your stories to each other, you come to know one another more deeply on a feeling level. Empathizing with the happy experiences of others can also increase your own happiness. Faith-sharing groups where members empathize can lead to rich and transforming experiences of the presence of God among those in the group.

DAILY PRACTICES

1. In your conversations with others, look for opportunities to empathize. Make sure you have been listening, validating, and clarifying. Here are several good opening phrases:

   A. "I've felt that way at times."

   B. "So you felt lonely (or some other feeling word). I know that feeling."

   C. "Lots of people feel (name an emotional state) at times. I know I have."

2. Watch the other person for signs that he or she is interested in hearing more about your experience. Be cautious about turning the conversation your way.

16

TAKING RISKS

In almost every discussion group there are usually one or two people in the crowd who seem to just sit back and say nothing. When they are asked to share their thoughts, feelings, and experiences, some of them are eager to talk. They just never felt that the moment was right — usually because the few extroverts in the group kept taking the floor every time there was half a second of silence. Very often, however, one of them may say something like this: "Oh, don't worry about me. I'm listening to everything and I'm enjoying it!"

Of course, group leaders are flattered that these silent participants are learning from the struggles of others. But they would prefer to have *everyone* join in the act. To know but not to be known is not their idea of how to improve relationships.

OBSTACLES TO RISKING

There are many reasons why people avoid taking risks, not the least of which is *fear*. You, for example, may be afraid because you have been hurt by others and don't want to be hurt again. But could it be that you are selfish and too lazy to put forth the energy to share yourself? Listed below are several of the most common statements which describe this fear. Each statement will be followed by an appropriate response.

1. "I just don't feel that I have anything worth saying. Nobody would be interested."
   Response: "Don't be foolish! How do *you* know what interests *me?* Anything you tell me about *you* will be interesting. I don't expect you to give me an expert's treatise on life; your sincere thoughts and feelings will do just fine."

2. "But if I really told you what I thought and felt, you might not understand."
   Response: "But then again I might. If I don't understand, I won't belittle you; I'll ask for clarification. And remember this: You probably don't have any unique thoughts and feelings — no matter how weird they may seem. They are unique for you, all right, but I've probably thought and felt the same things at times."

3. "Well, if people knew the real me, they might not like me."
   Response: "You know what? Most people will accept you if you tell them who you are; others won't care too much one way or another; and there may be a few characters who will reject you. So what are you going to do, let these emotional terrorists hold you hostage? You don't need their approval anyway, do you? The truth of the matter is that you don't really like yourself, and so you don't think you have anything that's really worth sharing. You've got some work to do on your own self-worth. But you can count on me: I'll do my part to love and accept you. Maybe this will help you believe in your *own* worth."

4. "I sometimes feel so mixed up that I don't know what'll come out if I start talking."
   Response: "So, what's new? You say you're mixed up right now — that you don't know what you really think or feel. I'm like that, too, sometimes. Maybe I can help you sort it out. I don't want a polished speech, you know — just the truth, the truth about you."

There are many other fear-based beliefs that can prevent you from risking. The point is that these beliefs limit your life experiences by keeping you lonely and uninvolved. When you experience the fear of risking and find these thoughts running through your mind, you need to practice some of the intrapersonal skills described in Part One: naming the feelings, identifying the life-limiting beliefs, confronting unhealthy beliefs and replacing them with healthy beliefs. That is what has been done in the statements and responses above. Daily examen provides another excellent opportunity to do this.

GROWING IN TRUST

If you briefly review the previous chapter you will note the natural connection between risking and empathizing. There is little risk involved in listening, validating, and clarifying, for your focus is entirely on the other person. With empathizing comes the opportunity to say something about yourself, and this can be frightening. But effective listening, validating, and clarifying can help you to discern whether it is safe to risk with other persons. If they are taking risks with you, it will be easier to open up with them.

While empathizing provides ideal opportunities to take risks, it nonetheless leaves the initiative with the other; and meantime you can do nothing until you believe it is relatively safe to do so. Real risk-taking requires that you sometimes take the initiative yourself.

Someone may ask the question, "How can I learn to trust others?" In answer, it can be said that trusting others is not a relationship skill, and so it cannot really be learned. Instead, trusting is a consequence of taking risks and finding acceptance. Of course, risking is easier with people you trust; but the paradox is that you cannot grow to trust others without also sharing something about yourself that is important to you.

Here, then, are a few equations that sum up these matters nicely:

- No risk, no acceptance by another.
- No acceptance by another, no trust.
- No trust, no deep communication.
- No deep communication, no intimacy.
- No intimacy, great loneliness.

- If you want intimacy (or at least don't want loneliness) you must risk.
- Nothing ventured, nothing gained.

DAILY PRACTICES

1. After reviewing your daily practices on pages 74-75, reflect on the individuals who belong in your first-level relationships.

    A. How often do each of these individuals communicate with you in a shaming manner? (Use the survey from page 74.)

    B. How do these shaming practices affect your willingness to risk?

    C. What are some of the ''no-talk'' areas for each of these individuals — topics that are too risky for you to discuss with them?

    D. With which individuals can you discuss specific topics that are risk areas for you?

2. Follow the above procedure as you reflect on your second-level relationships.

3. Be alert for opportunities to share yourself with others. Listed below are good opening phrases, which can spring from empathizing, or can be used to initiate a dialogue. Phrases are listed from least risky to most risky. Opening statements can be interchanged, of course.

    - ''Let me tell you what happened yesterday. Do you have a few moments?'' (Describe an experience; discuss behavior only.)
    - ''Would you like to know what I think about that?'' (Relate knowledge, ideas, and opinions.)
    - ''May I tell you my beliefs on this matter?'' (Refer in general to a disclosure of values.)
    - ''I'd like to tell you how I feel about this. Will you please listen?''

17

AFFIRMING OTHERS

One of the kindest deeds that can be done for others is to give them positive feedback. Chapter Eleven pointed out the danger of expressing a negative evaluation of another's personality and behavior; it is called *shaming*. This chapter focuses on its opposite, which is called *affirmation*.

AFFIRMATION PITFALLS

Affirmation means telling other people what you like about them as persons. If internalized by the other, the message is: "I'm good and lovable, and I have skills that are valued." This is the attitude that leads to happiness, so the importance of affirming others must not be underestimated.

Because affirmation is such a powerful force, it must be used wisely. If misused, it can do great harm, as the examples below illustrate.

1. **Giving positive feedback only when you want something from another is not affirmation but flattery.** This is cheap and manipulative — sometimes even evil! — for it is an attempt to control another's behavior to suit your own ends. You can usually tell when others are only flattering; their remarks seem hollow and frivolous.

2. **Telling other people that you love them only when they do nice things can lead them to conclude that you love them because of what they do and not for who they are.** This is conditional love, for it leads people to fall into the nasty habit of trying to earn love by doing nice things to please others. It is only natural, of course, that people experience loving feelings when others do nice things for them, but it is very important that they also know they are loved for who they *are* and not just for what they *do*. Tell them you love them and show them affection at all times, not just on special occasions.

3. **Affirmation that is not internalized can lead the other to become dependent on your approval.** "Did I do OK?" they seem to say as they return again and again to share experiences or demonstrate talents. Young children are especially prone to do this, but adults do it as well. The only way out of this trap is to help others internalize your affirmation. And a good way to do this is by asking what they value in the experience or project, and then validate them when they share this.

AFFIRMATION SKILLS

The above pitfalls can be eliminated by concentrating on the proper affirmation skills. It seems that many people do little affirming because they didn't see it modeled when they were growing up. Besides, it takes a bit of effort to affirm, because selfishness and laziness keep getting in the way. But this only points up the validity of considering affirmation a relationship skill which must be learned, practiced, and then put into use in your relationships. Listed below are a few ways this can be done.

1. **Quit taking other people and their actions for granted.** Be courteous. Say "Please" and "Thank you" when they perform their services for you, even if it is "their job."

2. **Express your love for others even in "bad" times and not just when things are going well.** Do this through words, hugs,

gifts, cards — whatever! How sad that your loved ones might die tonight without your having told them of your love lately.

3. **If you hear something nice said about someone, pass it on.**

4. **Comment positively on the pleasing things that other people do.** The more specific you can be, the better.

5. **Use a person's preferred name frequently when speaking with him or her.**

Developing an Affirming Attitude

Actually, the most effective affirmation is an intangible. In fact, all these affirmation skills will be empty techniques if you do not have an affirming attitude. People will know in short order if you're for them or against them, if you take them seriously or merely tolerate them, if you wish them happiness or couldn't care less. The paradox, again, is that an affirming attitude is strengthened by practicing affirming behaviors, and affirming behaviors are vitalized by affirming beliefs and feelings.

If you strive to become more affirming persons, your relationships will be strengthened within days. Everybody likes an affirmer, but how few there are in the world today! If you know at least one such person, you are fortunate indeed.

This writer has known a few affirmers during his lifetime. Two of them were college professors: Dr. Edmund D. Keiser, a herpetologist, and Dr. John W. Theiret, a botanist. They so loved their work that their students could not help but become enthused about lizards, snakes, and flowers when in their classrooms. Their enthusiasm opened up new worlds for their listeners, and their delight in teaching was so inherently affirming that students flocked to their classes.

This writer was further blessed in meeting people who were genuinely in love with God. One of them, Herman Sensat, affirmed him into conversion, discipleship, and mysticism. Herman died at the age of thirty-six in 1985, but he left behind a large group

of friends who loved more deeply because of his affirming attitude. At this moment, no doubt, he is getting a taste of his own
medicine — the bliss of eternal affirmation from his great, affirming God.

DAILY PRACTICES

1. Reflect on the people in your first-level relationships.

   A. What are some things that these people do regularly which
   please you? List at least five items for each person. Be
   specific.

   B. How often do you comment positively on these pleasing
   experiences?

   C. Examine some of the suggestions for affirming described
   in this chapter. Which of these can you utilize more often to
   affirm your loved ones?

2. Follow these same procedures as you reflect on the people in
   your second-level relationships.

3. Look for ways to affirm people more often — even complete
   strangers. But don't try to be a total affirmer in one day. Take it
   easy! People will think you're a phony if you come at them too
   strongly, and they may be right. One or two more affirming
   remarks from you each day will soon add up. Use your daily
   examen to become more aware of opportunities to affirm.

18

ASSERTING YOUR NEEDS

Many people are learning about assertiveness in today's world. Several popular books tell people how to say "no" without feeling guilty. At numerous lectures and workshops, assertive parenting, assertive discipline, and even emotional assertiveness are being discussed. And more than a few corporations are beginning to feature training in assertiveness skills.

Why this sudden concern about assertiveness? Practical people have come to realize that asserting is a valid relationship skill which should be taught, learned, and practiced.

How is this skill described? *Asserting refers to a person's right to state his or her thoughts, feelings, and desires.*

The reason so many are attracted to assertiveness programs is because many of them have spent a lifetime denying themselves the right to state their own needs. They have learned to be indirect in asking for their needs, or else they try to manipulate others into meeting them by playing silly games. For example, they say that a good supervisor at work is one who can get his employees to believe that his goals are really their own ideas. And a popular book of some few years back *(The Total Woman,* Revell, 1973) proved to be simply a manifesto on ways in which wives can get what they want by manipulating their husbands. In the long run, however, these indirect and controlling strategies cause more problems than they solve.

OBSTACLES TO ASSERTIVENESS

Many people find it difficult to assert their needs directly. As usual, there are distorted beliefs and assumptions underlying their fears. Here are a few of them with an answer for each.

1. "It would be selfish for me to state my needs."

   Response: "Really? You expect others to tell you *their* needs so you can love them as they need to be loved; but you won't tell them *your* needs so they can return the gift. You want only to give but not to receive? Who do you think you are? Are you too proud to be loved?"

   If this is your problem, perhaps you are confusing selfishness with self-love. You are being selfish when you pursue your wants/needs to the detriment of yourself and others. But there are many ways to let others know your wants/needs without being selfish. And if loving others is really your concern, know that by loving yourself you are better able to love others.

2. "But I shouldn't even have to state my wants/needs. If other people loved me, they would know what I want/need."

   Response: "No. That is not true. Even after decades of marriage, it is still necessary for spouses to state their needs to one another. Your brooding in self-pity only confuses other people and makes you play silly games."

   Many times people do not give you what you need simply because they do not know about it. If you do not ask, you cannot expect to receive. Suppose — in order to make ends meet — you needed a raise at work. If you do not ask for it, your employer will presume that you do not need it.

3. "I'm afraid if I state my thoughts, feelings, and needs, people will ridicule me."

   Response: "This was dealt with in Chapter Sixteen. If others ridicule you, give them a good "I message" to tell them how you feel about their immature response. If they persist, leave them alone.''

4. ''Sometimes when I assert myself, it upsets people, and I hate a scene.''

Response: ''So what's the alternative? Is it really more pleasant to deny yourself the right to be heard? Is life better under the doormat, where you brood in an effort to avoid controversy?''

People who frequently reject your reasonable requests are probably more interested in controlling you than loving you. You'd better take a good, hard look at that relationship and what needs to happen if you are to grow in it.

5. ''I'm afraid the other will say 'no' to my request.''

Response: ''This could happen, of course; but remember that asserting is different from demanding. Asserting leaves the other free to say 'no.' ''

If you cannot live with a ''no'' answer, then you need to move into a confronting or negotiating stance (which will be treated in the next two chapters).

6. ''Sometimes I feel so angry and frustrated about my needs that I'm afraid I'll come across as aggressive.''

Response: ''That is a risk that has to be taken. The other alternatives are repressing your needs or playing silly games to try to manipulate people into meeting your needs; but both of these are unhealthy. So long as you avoid shaming others and threatening them personally, you will be able to stay out of harmful aggressiveness.''

ASSERTIVENESS SKILLS

Many relationships go awry because the parties involved try to control each other in different ways. Assertiveness can help you do your part to break through some of this manipulation. In practicing this skill, there is one simple rule: honesty for the sake of love. This honesty is the enemy of control and manipulation. Let yourself live in this light.

Here are two ways of asserting yourself:

1. "I would like this (a specific behavior) because of that (a specific value/need). Will you please do this?"

2. "Would you be willing to do this (a specific behavior)? This would help me to do that (a specific need)."

Note that in each case you are requesting specific behavior. A husband cannot ask his wife to be more caring, but he can ask her to cook his favorite meal. Parents cannot ask their children to be nice, but they can ask them to take turns playing with their toys.

In asking for your needs, it is important that you not sound demanding. Your tone of voice should not be harsh, but polite and respectful. People are more likely to respond to this approach and you are more likely to get what you need.

REFUSAL SKILLS

This chapter has thus far treated assertiveness from a positive stance of asking for your needs. But this skill can also be used to set boundaries, or to state what you *don't* want. For many, many people, setting personal boundaries is a major issue in personal growth.

If, for example, you are asked to do something you don't really want to do, you can assert your preference not to do it. Simply say: "I would rather not do that (mention the specific behavior)" or "I would rather not do that (mention the specific behavior) because of this (mention conflict with your schedule, values, your own needs)." If the other cannot accept your response, then it is on to confrontation and negotiation — if you are willing.

The skill of assertiveness as request and/or refusal is especially important in the area of sexuality. In marriage, for example, partners will find that accommodations in this area will be necessary. Asserting yourself honestly in love means that you have the right to say: "I would rather not tonight because I need some time alone." At this, a loving partner should validate and empathize, then leave you alone. But if your partner continues to demand, you may choose to accommodate in different ways — out of love or out of resentment — or you may persist in your assertive refusal stance. The point here is that the choice of how to share your sexuality is yours.

Asserting yourself is one way of letting others know that you value yourself as a person. If you have respect for yourself, it is more likely that others will respect you, too.

DAILY PRACTICES

1. With which of the obstacles to assertiveness did you most identify in this chapter? How does this obstacle manifest itself in your relationships?

2. What are some of the needs you have been afraid to ask for? Make a list, then envision yourself asking politely, while using the skills recommended in this chapter.

3. Are you honest with others in telling them your thoughts, feelings, desires, and expectations — especially concerning your wants/needs? Do not leave them guessing. Let them know, too, what you think and feel about their demands upon you.

19

Confronting Unacceptable Behavior

People learn much about who you are by the manner in which you respond to them. They may also consider your past accomplishments or the recommendations of friends, but your personal relationships with others will hinge on the manner in which you respond to them and they to you. If you listen to them, take them seriously, validate their feelings, empathize with their experiences, and affirm the good you see, they will learn that you are a warm and loving person. They will also learn about your own self-respect by noting whether or not you assert your thoughts and expectations appropriately, and if you confront them when necessary.

You are constantly teaching people about how they may relate with you. A wife who allows her husband to abuse her physically and emotionally for years has taught him that it's OK for him to dominate, manipulate, and take advantage of her in whatever way he wishes. This example is not so extreme, as some may imagine. There are many people who are willing to dominate you if you let them. It's the great scourge of relationships, this tendency to try to control others. But if you are sincerely interested in growing in love, you must do your part to break this cycle of evil. That's where confronting comes into play.

CONFRONTATION SKILLS

Confrontation means telling another what you dislike about his or her actions. It differs from assertion which focuses on your *own* thoughts, expectations, and behaviors, while confrontation focuses on the *other's*. It also differs from shaming by focusing *only* on behavior, rather than on personality. Shaming says, "I don't like what you're doing and I don't like you either!" Confronting says, "I like you — that's not the issue with me; the issue is what you're doing right now." It is only by confronting that you cease to accept what you consider inappropriate behavior.

How do you confront others without putting them down or driving them away? In Chapter Two you learned to use the "I message" which communicates three pieces of information: a) the nature of the issue; b) your feelings about the issue; and c) the consequences to you and/or others. There are different ways of expressing this information, but here is one example.

"I feel sad (or some other feeling word) about what happened (the issue) because so many persons have been hurt (the consequences)."

People receiving an "I message" from you gain several valuable pieces of information. First of all, they learn that you are taking responsibility for your own feelings rather than making others responsible for them. (A "you message" blames the other person; for example, "You make me so mad.") Secondly, they learn that you are not interested in putting them down through name-calling (which shaming does). Thirdly, they discover how their behavior is affecting you so that, fourthly, they can perhaps learn something about how they can love you better. They also learn that you are not a doormat, and that you care enough about yourself and your relationship with them to challenge growth.

The above information deals with your confrontation of others when their behavior affects you personally. But it is also appropriate to confront others when their behavior has no immediate impact upon you — when, in fact, the only danger is to themselves (and others). But you should be careful not to confuse loving confrontation with meddling. There are many instances when a loving person should confront the behavior of others, as the two examples below illustrate.

1. When you see a parent shaming his or her child you can say: "I get angry when I see you calling your child names and hitting her. How do you think she feels about what you just did?"

2. In the case of alcohol abuse (or similar abuses) you can say: "I'm concerned about your drinking, good buddy. It looks to me as though you've been hurting yourself quite a lot lately."

You should react in a similar manner when you note dishonesty at work and in government because confronting says "I care about you."

If you saw a person backing toward the edge of a cliff, wouldn't you yell "Stop"? Surely you wouldn't turn your back and walk away, claiming that it's none of your business and that you don't want to be meddling. This need for confronting others — out of loving concern for their own good — can happen quite frequently.

USE OF DISCIPLINE

Unfortunately, it is also sometimes necessary to let others know what you plan to do if their behavior does not change. This combination of confrontation plus sanctions (punishments) is what is meant by disciplining.

Usually disciplining is thought of as something adults do with children, but it is obvious that it can happen between adults as well. Disciplining is another way of telling people what you are willing to live with and what you will not tolerate. In order for your disciplining to be effective, however, you must be creative in using sanctions. A good rule of thumb is to try to establish a link between the sanction and a value at stake. Several examples are listed below, each of which could follow an "I message."

1. (One spouse to another): "I feel hurt and angry when you yell and curse at me while we're talking. I can't communicate when

you do this. If you don't stop, I'm going to walk away and we can finish this later, when you can talk to me more civilly.''

2. (Wife to husband): "If you don't stop abusing me and the children, we're leaving. We can't live in this constant fear.''

3. (Parent to a child): "I can't understand what you're saying when you keep whining the way you do, so I'm going to sit you in this chair so you can calm down a bit. When you've stopped your crying, I'll come talk to you.''

4. (Employer to a worker who is often tardy): "If you don't come to work on time, I'll find someone who will.''

5. (Mother to children): "There'll be no watching television and no treats until this work is done and your rooms are put in order.''

You see, then, that confrontation through the "I message" approach is often not enough to motivate others to change their behavior. Adding a creative sanction is sometimes necessary as well; it's another way of influencing loving behaviors in others.

DAILY PRACTICES

1. After reviewing your journal responses to the drills on pages 74 and 94, reflect on individuals who belong in your first-level relationships.

   A. Which specific shaming practices from others do you need to confront?

   B. Write out "I message" confrontations for specific shaming incidents that have taken place recently and which will likely take place again. Include statements about sanctions where necessary.

C. Imagine you are experiencing one of these incidents again. See the other's face; feel the hurt and anger within you as you are shamed; see yourself confronting by using the "I message" statements you've written out; let the other know what sanctions you will impose if necessary; feel now the satisfaction of knowing that you've done your part to make the relationship better. The "ball" is now in the other person's court.

2. Repeat this process with your second-level relationships.

3. Using your knowledge of affirming others who please you, now turn your attention to confronting those who displease you. Not all at once, though, or else you'll come across as self-righteous. Use the "I message" approach when an incident happens. Ordinary life presents sufficient opportunities for practicing confrontation. Add sanctions if it seems you're getting nowhere.

20

LEARNING TO NEGOTIATE

John, a newlywed, comes home from work one day only to find
that Marsha, his wife who also works, has not washed the dishes
and has not started supper. (Both John and Marsha have been to
several communication workshops, so they know how to use the
skills discussed in this book. Even so, see what can happen.)

John *(walking out of the kitchen into the living room where
Marsha sits reading the paper)*: Marsha, what's with all these
dirty dishes? And what's for supper? I'm starving!

Marsha *(glancing up in annoyance at being disturbed)*: I just
didn't get around to it yet. I'm tired right now, and I need a rest.

John *(realizing for the first time that the honeymoon is over)*:
You need a rest and *I* need some food. And *we* both need a clean
kitchen.

Marsha: That's right, John. And right now I'm taking care of
my need. If your need is so urgent, then I suggest you take care
of it, too.

John: Are you suggesting that I cook supper and do the dishes?

Marsha: If you've got to have it your way just at this moment,
then that's exactly what I'm suggesting. If you can wait a while,
I'll take care of it. Now I'd like to get back to my article if you
don't mind.

John *(completely unnerved)*: But, Marsha, it's *your* job to cook
and clean. I *can't* do those things.

Marsha *(really angry now)*: Well then you'll have to *learn*, because I don't intend to be a kitchen slave for the rest of my life.

John: But cooking and cleaning are women's work — women's work!

Marsha: Who says? Who says?

Stalemate! Despite the fact that John and Marsha used listening, validating, clarifying, asserting, and confronting skills, they still reached a stalemate.

At this point in the dialogue, three options are open to John and Marsha:

1. **Ordinary pressure.** John might add, "If you don't cook my supper now, I'm going to go eat out somewhere without you."

   Marsha might reply: "Fine! I told you to do what you needed to do to meet your need. But if you don't let me rest a while now, I'll have to go to sleep early, and I'll be a wreck this evening when your parents come to visit."

2. **Breakdown.** John might keep on trying to impose his will on Marsha with Marsha responding in like manner. This controlling pressure may be exerted by saying that the other is not a good spouse (verbal abuse). Other possibilities include the "cold shoulder" and the various kinds of acting-out and shaming.

3. **Negotiation.** John and Marsha might find this an opportune time to discuss their expectations of one another regarding kitchen duties.

TYPES OF EXPECTATIONS

In any relationship — professional as well as personal — there are times when it is necessary to negotiate expectations. You change, your mutual situation changes, and therefore the manner in which you take responsibility for the current situation changes. If you do not learn to renegotiate your expectations constantly, there will be a breakdown in the relationship, with each partner trying to control the other.

There are two broad categories of expectations: covert and overt. *Covert* expectations are those which you are aware of in a vague manner but which you have not discussed. John's expectation that Marsha should cook supper because that is a woman's job is one such example. *Overt* expectations are more explicit. They are expectations that you have a right to because you have talked them over with the other person, and you agreed upon them. If Marsha had at some time in the past agreed that she would do the dishes and cook supper, then John would have a right to confront her about this — unless they never made it clear *when* Marsha would do this (before or after resting a bit on returning from work).

You will usually get in trouble with your covert expectations when they carry with them a multitude of ''shoulds'' and because they are loaded with energy from the unconscious. (You don't have them, they have you.) No doubt, John is pretty emotional in his belief that cooking and cleaning are women's work. His mother and father probably taught him this in their modeling, and it was reinforced by Church and society in general. All these lessons contributed to John's unconscious attitudes about men and women — attitudes which he now brings to his marriage and imposes on Marsha. Undoubtedly, Marsha has covert expectations of her own which will ''surprise'' John — especially during their first year of marriage and after they have their first child. Good marriage preparation helps, but these ''surprises'' cannot be completely eliminated.

NEGOTIATION: A FOUR-STEP PROCESS

Negotiating calls for making your expectations clear, then taking steps to reach agreement on your expectations. There are several movements in this process, which are described below. Of course, progression through this process is enhanced when people practice all the other relationship skills discussed in the previous chapters of this book.

1. **Identification of the issue and the expectations you bring to this issue.** "What are we arguing about? And why?" "What do I want? What do you want?" The more specific you can be, the better. John and Marsha were just beginning to do this in the example given above.

2. **Identification of the values implicit in the expectations.** In other words, what is the purpose of a specific expectation? What need is it addressing? From which moral principles was it derived? Is it overt or covert material?

3. **Examination of alternative ways to realize these values, needs, and principles at stake.** Brainstorm your ideas. Be open to new ways.

4. **Reaching agreement on new expectations with which both parties can live.** This is accomplished in one of two ways:

   • *By compromising:* Each person gives up something he or she wants in order to reach an agreement because there is more to be gained in the agreement than in stubborn isolation. This is different from "doormatting" or compromising simply to avoid controversy.
   • *By synthesizing:* Each person incorporates the other's ideas and expectations into an agreement which embodies the values of both.

If negotiation does not result in a new compromise or synthesis, then the stalemate will continue. The possibility of breakdown then becomes stronger than ever.

This negotiating process is not only a healthy way to reach agreements concerning responsibilities in a relationship, but it is also a good way to settle business and governmental disagreements and arguments of opinion. In the case of arguments of opinion, negotiating would call for both parties to first clear away semantic difficulties by agreeing on the meaning of certain critical words.

Next comes examination of the premises and assumptions which underpin the different opinions. Finally, both parties may either arrive at a new synthesis from what they've learned, or they may choose to agree to disagree about certain matters.

DAILY PRACTICES

1. After reviewing your Daily Practices from previous Chapters Eleven, Sixteen, and Nineteen, reflect on your first-level relationships.

   A. Which expectations imposed on you by others do you need to confront and renegotiate?

   B. Are any of your expectations of others covert? Unreasonable? In need of renegotiation?

   C. Take a risk and be assertive in inviting the other to renegotiate expectations. Use the four-step process described in this chapter.

   - Take only one issue at a time.
   - Start with something not too controversial.
   - Celebrate your new agreements and wait a while before opening another negotiation. Good relationships come in many small steps and not large, dramatic ones.
   - If you and your partner experience a breakdown in negotiation — especially concerning a serious issue — ask for help. One of the purposes of counseling and consultation is to help facilitate negotiation in relationships.

2. Use these same steps with a second-level relationships.

21

FORGIVING FROM THE HEART

In the process of practicing relationship skills, there is one thing you can be sure of: You are going to fall short from time to time. Even after years of consciously trying to love God and other people, your attitudes and behavior will — on occasion — degenerate to patterns characteristic of a spoiled three-year-old. Far too often, you hurt other people during these times. When this happens, you need to seek forgiveness that you might go on loving.

OBSTACLES TO FORGIVENESS

Of all the relationship skills discussed in this book, forgiveness is the most difficult to practice. In the first place, to say that you are sorry goes against the grain of your lower, selfish nature; then, too, you probably haven't known too many models of forgiveness during your lives. Furthermore, there are a few common misconceptions which prevent you from ever discovering the meaning of true forgiveness. Here are a few, along with an answer to each.

1. "If I forgive other people for the wrongs done to me, it is the same as telling them that I approve of their actions."
   Response: "No, not really! Jesus never approves of wrongdoing. 'Go and sin no more' is his counsel. It is possible, then,

to let others know that you have been hurt by their actions but that you forgive them anyway.''

2. ''Asking another person to forgive me is just a way of seeking their approval.''
   Response: ''Yes, that can be a legitimate danger. But gaining the other's approval is not the reason you seek forgiveness. You do so in order to own up to the consequences of your actions.''

3. ''Asking another to forgive me is self-debasing. I feel like I'm groveling.''
   Response: ''True, seeking forgiveness does have a way of humbling the proud ego. This is not the same as groveling, however. You do it because of a loving principle and not to get something out of another.''

4. ''Forgiveness doesn't change anything. What's done is done!''
   Response: ''Forgiveness *does* change things. It changes your attitude about what has happened, and that's *something!*''

5. ''Love means never having to say you're sorry.''
   Response: ''This one has been disproved many times. Yet it's not at all a naïve statement. In fact, it comes very close to the true meaning of forgiveness in its implication that lovers simply overlook the wrongs done against them — almost as if no wrong had ever been done. Even so, it is healthy to apologize for wrongs done — at least for the sake of humility and responsibility.''

FREEDOM AND HEALING

What is meant by forgiveness, then? The essence of forgiveness consists of holding nothing against another. God's perfect forgiveness is exemplified in Psalm 103:12: ''As far as the east is from the west, so far has he put our transgressions from us.'' This attitude allows a relationship to continue to grow after wrongs have been committed.

There are two sides to forgiveness: yours and theirs. Forgiving others means that you let them know that you hold nothing against them; seeking forgiveness means doing your part to ask others to hold nothing against you.

The value of forgiveness can best be appreciated by noting the consequences of its neglect. When you do wrong to others, you naturally try to rid yourself of the unpleasant emotional energy spawned by the hurt. Sometimes this makes you brood and sulk about it, or, worse, you may begin plotting how to balance the scales of justice by some kind of retaliation. Then begins the vicious cycle of negative thoughts and feelings, which ultimately distorts your perceptions and produces harmful behavior. One of the tactics of the devil (see Ephesians 6:11) is to stoke the fires of retribution, manipulation, and control, all of which feed on the hurts you have experienced. Where these attitudes finally bear fruit in retribution, there is the potential for a cycle of violence which may never be terminated.

It is a brave and humble (and also practical) soul who finally says, "Enough! These venomous thoughts are killing me, and they're destroying us. I, for my part, apologize for (here list specific words and deeds) that I have done. I will prove my sincerity by refraining from doing these things again. (This is called a firm resolve to sin no more.) I'll negotiate new expectations with you, and I'll even undertake specific disciplines to help me behave more responsibly (this is what is meant by doing penance). So will you forgive me my part in our situation? Will you no longer hold these wrongs against me?"

COMMON PROBLEMS

Several questions may arise at this point. Here they are — with suggested responses.

1. "What if the other says no? What if my apology is not accepted?"

    Response: "Never mind. You've done your part, although you must also make restitution if that is needed. Now you must get on with the process of healing so that you can break free from the chains of resentment that have been stifling your growth. Praying for the well-being of your 'enemy' is an excellent way to break free.''

2. "But what if the other continues to treat me badly?"

   Response: "Then you need to do something practical — like distancing yourself from such a person. Being tied to what you abhor — according to Buddha — is one of the many sources of human misery. Christ also tells us to treat those who persist in wrongdoing as tax collectors and sinners — which, to a Jew, meant leaving them alone. The extremes here are giving up on the relationship too early, or banging your head against a wall until you lose your mind. Get help in discernment if you must."

3. "What if the other seeks forgiveness from me first?"

   Response: "You must forgive others 'seventy times seven,' said Jesus, which means every time they seek forgiveness."

4. "But what if the other keeps doing me wrong and just seems to be using forgiveness to manipulate me?"

   Response: "Keep right on forgiving but also continue to practice asserting, confronting, and negotiating. If these don't work, seek help through counseling. If that doesn't work, then forgive the other and move on. Forgiveness does not mean that you have to live in a situation where you are abused. It simply means that you hold nothing against the other while taking practical steps to do what is necessary for your own personal growth."

5. "What if the other has hurt me but has not sought forgiveness? Should I take the initiative in the forgiving process?"

   Response: "It is not a good idea to tell people they are forgiven unless they ask for it. Forgiveness is not a substitute for confrontation, nor, worse, should it be a *means* of confrontation. If another has hurt you, confront first, then express forgiveness if an apology is offered. If no apology is offered, however, you must forgive in your heart and pray for this person, then treat him or her as if it is all behind you." (The situation with children is different in that children should be taught forgiving skills after confronting them.)

DAILY PRACTICES

1. After reviewing your earlier Daily Practices, reflect on your first-level relationships.

   A. Recall any of your past behaviors that need apologies.

- Think of creative ways to apologize (by card, letter, gift, phone call, whatever).
- Be sure somewhere to give the message: "I apologize for (mention specific behaviors) and I regret that you were hurt (here list specific ways you know the other was hurt)." Let the other know that you will be careful about this in the future.
- Make practical restitution, if necessary (return money, repair or replace damaged property, whatever).

   B. Recall the specific behavior of others that still needs your forgiveness.

- If you have not confronted them concerning these matters, then do so — at least the next chance you get.
- Accept their forgiveness if it is offered.
- Pray for the grace to no longer hold these things against them.

2. Follow the same process for your second-level relationships.

3. Do not wait until wrongs accumulate, but begin apologizing and making amends as soon as you become aware of hurting others.

22

BRINGING IT ALL
TOGETHER

In workshops or lectures, any description of the relationship skills described in this book usually receive the following comment during the discussion period: "This all makes sense, but it's surely a lot to remember. In fact, it's too much!"

What is ironic is that the people who make such remarks have mastered far more complex skills through the years. Many of them have learned to drive automobiles, to program computers, to type, to learn a new language, to read and write, and to do arithmetic. At first they probably did these things awkwardly and with many mistakes. In time, however, the skills became appropriated into the unconscious as habitual ways of behaving. The same can happen with the relationship skills, although most persons will probably first have to change some of their life-long ideas about relationships in general.

But perhaps there's more behind people's complaints than the issue of too many skills to master. Maybe these complaints are saying something about the value placed on relationships. People don't seem to mind spending thousands of dollars to learn new skills for making a living. Are you, for instance, a bit reluctant to learn more about relationship skills? Could it be that you think you know enough already — that you've already mastered this field? Or are you by some chance marked with those ridiculous social stigmas which hold that those who go to personal growth workshops must be a little disorganized in their living process? In either case there is a baffling paradox here: Everyone seems to recognize the connection between quality relationships and happiness, but they're generally unwilling to do anything to improve their relationships until they are forced to do so.

IMPORTANCE OF
LOVING SERVICE
AND DAILY EXAMEN

How, then, do you put it all together? How do you use these skills in an appropriate manner? Any general guidelines for using relationship skills could certainly be invalidated by some particular situation or circumstances. Rather than guidelines, then, a proper focusing of these skills is attained through the attitude of loving service, and the discipline of daily conscious examen.

The attitude of *loving service* must be cultivated by calling to mind the following questions during an interpersonal encounter:

1. "What's happening with the other person?" (To find out what the person is saying, thinking, feeling, doing, expecting, use your skills of listening, validating, clarifying, and empathizing.)

2. "What does the other need me to say or do?" (Again, you might respond with listening skills, but you might also choose to affirm, confront, or forgive.)

3. "What do I need the other to do for me?" (You might ask to be listened to, or you might risk by asserting, confronting, or proposing negotiation or forgiveness.)

4. "What do the other person and I need to do together?" (A mutual exchange of all the skills is one possibility — as in a good, informal, spontaneous discussion. Here, too, negotiating and forgiving will come into play.)

Calling to mind these four questions will not make you more anxious and awkward during a conversation. If anything, it will make you less anxious. Most conversational anxiety is spawned by thoughts such as, "I wonder what this person thinks about me?" and "I hope I'm coming across OK." These thoughts are self-centered. But three of the four questions focus your attention on the other or on your relationship. The third question is, of course, concerned with self; it is only when this question is taken out of the context of the other three that anxiety will be increased.

The loving service questions help you to recognize when it is appropriate to employ a specific relationship skill. A similar situation exists when you drive a car. "Am I obeying the traffic laws?" you ask yourself. Depending on the answer to this question, you may choose to apply the brakes, shift gears, or even change lanes. The skill to be used depends on the situation, and the question helps to understand the situation. All skills lose their meaning when viewed as ends in themselves. It is only by asking the right questions that you come to recognize the appropriate times to use specific skills. This holds true in your relationships and in other areas of life as well.

The discipline of *daily examen* is the second strategy recommended for helping you to integrate your relationship skills. You learned this process in Chapter Ten. If you have been doing your daily examen, you already know about the many ways it can help you to focus your energies more effectively in the service of love. The examen provides an excellent process for looking back over your day to see how you have used your skills. Were you talking when you should have been listening? Did you miss opportunities to affirm? In short, the examen allows you to affirm your progress, note your failures, and resolve to do better next time.

Persistence

One final suggestion: Hang in there and stay with it. You've learned harder skills during your lifetime, but few more important than these. And don't be too hard on yourself. Be more concerned about making progress rather than seeking the ideal of perfection. Read these chapters over every now and then, and find other books that discuss these skills. If possible, join a group of some kind to support your efforts. And when everything seems complicated, simplify. But don't ever stray from loving service and the daily examen. These two disciplines will help you to continue to make progress in everything presented in this book.

DAILY PRACTICES

1. Are you now convinced that relationship skills are important in your life?

2. Write out a short sketch of the first part of this book.

3. Now write out a sketch of the second part of this book.

4. Make a special effort to note if you were calling to mind the four questions of loving service while you were relating to another person. If you were, then chances are very good that you employed the relationship skills appropriately. If you were not, then that is probably why you misused the skills.

Support Group Format

1. **Gathering:** Allow about ten minutes for people to come together, find their places, and settle in.

2. **Opening:** Allow five minutes for prayer, song, inspirational reading.

3. **Discussion time:** 30-60 minutes. Use option A or B.

   A. Sharing experiences.

   - What have been some of the joys and struggles in your life recently?
   - Which of the relationship skills discussed in this book have you been working to improve recently?
   - What insights from journal work and examen would you like to share with this group?
   - What would you like to learn about relationship skills from other group members? Ask for feedback.

   B. Study Meeting. Do one of the following.

   - Read one or more chapters from the book together, and then ask: a) Does everyone agree with the information presented? b) Will someone provide examples from his or her life?
   - Have a group member give a presentation on one or more relationship skills. Discuss.

- Have a group member give a review of another book which deals with relationships. Discuss.
- Watch a film or video which discusses relationships. Discuss.

4. **Closure.** Allow five minutes for this. "At this meeting, I learned . . ."

5. **Announcements** for next meeting.

Lessons In Loving
Workshops and Lectures

Philip St. Romain is the director of Personal Growth Services, Inc., a nonprofit organization that offers workshops, lectures, and retreats on a variety of topics. For more information, write Personal Growth Services, Inc., 13586 Neil Avenue, Baton Rouge, LA 70810. Phone: 504/766-7615.

SUGGESTED READING

Berne, Eric, M.D. *Games People Play,* Ballantine Books, 1964.

Buscaglia, Leo. *Love,* Fawcett, 1972.

Carnegie, Dale. *How to Win Friends and Influence People,* (Pocket) Simon and Schuster, 1936.

Gardner, Howard. *Frames of Mind: The Theory of Multiple Intelligences,* Basic Books, 1983.

Jamplosky, Gerald G., M.D. *Love Is Letting Go of Fear,* Celestial Arts, 1979.

Laz, Medard. *The Six Levels of a Happy Marriage,* Liguori Publications, 1978.

Peck, M. Scott, M.D. *The Road Less Traveled: A New Psychology of Love, Traditional Values, and Spiritual Growth,* Simon and Schuster, 1978.

Powell, John, S.J. *Why Am I Afraid to Tell You Who I Am?* Argus Communications, 1969.

Powell, John, S.J. *The Secret of Staying in Love,* Argus Communications, 1974.

Osborne, Cecil G. *The Art of Getting Along With People,* Zondervan Books, 1980.

St. Romain, Philip. *Building Character in Young People,* Pelican Publications, 1986.

St. Romain, Philip. *Pathways to Serenity,* Liguori Publications, 1988.